Michael Ondaatje:
Word, Image, Imagination

Michael Ondaatje: Word, Image, Imagination

by Leslie Mundwiler

Talonbooks • Vancouver • 1984

for Paul Feyerabend in appreciation

Copyright © 1984 Leslie Mundwiler

Published with assistance from the Canada Council.
This book has been published with the help of
a grant from the Canadian Federation for the Humanities,
using funds provided by the Social Sciences and Humanities
Research Council of Canada.

TALONBOOKS
201 1019 East Cordova
Vancouver
British Columbia v6A 1M8
Canada

Text designed and typeset at The Coach House Press, Toronto
Printed in Canada by Hignell Printing Limited
First printing: August 1984

CANADIAN CATALOGUING IN PUBLICATION DATA

Mundwiler, Leslie, 1944 -
Michael Ondaatje

(The New Canadian criticism series)
Includes index.
ISBN 0-88922-216-9

1. Ondaatje, Michael, 1943- —Criticism and interpretation.
I. Title. II. Series.
PS 8529.N39Z78 1984 C818'.5409 C84-091452-0
PR 9199.3.0 52Z78 1984

Contents

Abbreviations

Passages from Michael Ondaatje's writings have been taken from the following editions:

BK   *The Collected Works of Billy the Kid.*
         Toronto: House of Anansi, 1970.

CS   *Coming Through Slaughter.* Toronto: House
         of Anansi, 1976.

DM   *The Dainty Monsters.* Toronto: The Coach
         House Press, 1967.

MWST   *The Man with Seven Toes.* Toronto: The
         Coach House Press, 1969.

RF   *Running in the Family.* Toronto: McClelland
         and Stewart, 1982.

RJ   *Rat Jelly.* Toronto: The Coach House Press, 1973.

TK   *There's a Trick with a Knife I'm Learning to Do.*
         Toronto: McClelland and Stewart, 1979.

Introduction

THE critical discussion offered here does not attempt to interpret Michael Ondaatje's work in terms of biography or literary debts. In a 1975 interview Ondaatje indicated dissatisfaction with these approaches, "emotional or psychological rightness" being more important for him than the factuality of biographical reference, while the question of influences was, apparently, largely irrelevant. I have not given an evaluation of the place of Ondaatje's work in our culture although I believe this would be valuable. What have been the apparent social determinants of his choice of subject matters? How has the publication of his work fitted into the institutional and economic character of Canadian publishing? What institutions and social formations are represented by Ondaatje's reviewers and critics? Answers to such questions with respect to his work and that of his contemporaries would go a long way toward providing an analysis of the state of the arts at this point in our cultural history. Since this study proceeds along other lines, a summary of his literary and filmmaking career, with some consideration of his methods of work and of publishing and production details, is given here.[1]

*

Ondaatje in Outline. Philip Michael Ondaatje was born in Colombo, Ceylon (now Sri Lanka), September 12, 1943. Before his first return visit to the island in 1978, the published work involved few references to his childhood in that setting. The important exceptions were the poems "Dates" and "Letters & Other Worlds" (both from *Rat Jelly*) and "Light," all three coming in the mid-Seventies after he had established himself as a writer. In response to a query about Ceylon's influence on the first book, *The Dainty Monsters*, Ondaatje remarked,

It is there I suppose, but not in any conscious way. There are a couple of poems which refer to images of Ceylon, but mostly I was concerned with coming to terms with the present landscape of that time.[2]

9

This preoccupation with the present, with immediacy, even in work which ostensibly draws upon the past, has only given way in recent years – and then only somewhat – with Ondaatje's recollection and exploration of the Ceylon background.

Ondaatje moved to London at age 11 and finished his preparatory schooling at Dulwich College. By his own account, he did not begin writing poetry until he came to Canada at age 19, in 1962. Considering the arduous apprenticeships of poets like Al Purdy and Milton Acorn, it is rather remarkable that Ondaatje published four books of poetry by age 30. He has given credit for the initial impetus to "meeting poets and having enthusiastic teachers," singling out the influence of Arthur Motyer of Bishop's University. About Motyer's approach to teaching, Ondaatje has said,

It was a very theatrical thing or presentation of a poem. He also taught drama and he read beautifully. He'd come into class and read a Browning poem and the poem became an acted thing, a passionate thing.[3]

But part of the credit for Ondaatje's development as a poet must also go to the special relationship between the universities and high art, which has had tremendous importance for the directions of literature in the post-World-War-II period. He lived within this relationship by pursuing a career as a university teacher while developing as a writer.

Ondaatje received a BA from the University of Toronto (after earlier studies at Bishop's) and, in 1968, an MA from Queen's University. His MA thesis was titled "Mythology in the Poetry of Edwin Muir: A Study in the Making and Using of Mythology in Edwin Muir's Poetry" and signaled a central preoccupation of his thought as an artist. "I am interested in myth," Ondaatje emphasized in a 1972 interview;

Making it, remaking it, exploding. I don't like poems or works that cash in on a cliché of history of a personality. I don't like pop westerns and pop Billy the Kids. Myths are only of value to me when they are realistic as well as having other qualities of myth. Another thing that interests me about myth is how and when figures get caught in myths.[4]

He taught at University of Western Ontario over 1967-1971, but in 1971, he was fired by the university because he would not do a Ph.D. He had published to that point three books of poetry and a critical study of Leonard Cohen as well as producing "Sons of Captain Poetry," a film about the work of bpNichol. Two days after the firing it was announced that he would receive the Governor-General's Award for *The Collected Works of Billy the Kid*. The university-high art symbiosis had failed – perhaps because, from the artist's standpoint, it has never been a true symbiosis, more like an uncertain marriage of convenience. Ondaatje returned to the university, however – to teach at Glendon College in Toronto where, since 1971, he has been a member of the English faculty.

Over the Sixties Ondaatje's main efforts as an artist were given to poetry. His first published book, *The Dainty Monsters* (1967), was a selection of work largely taken from the 1963-1966 period. He has acknowledged the editorial assistance of George Whalley ("in the structuring of the book") and of Wayne Clifford ("in the final editing").[5] The success of the first book, where reviewers were concerned, was anticipated by the prior appearance of most of the poems in prestigious literary magazines and by the anthologizing of a few in *Modern Canadian Verse, Penguin Book of Canadian Verse, Commonwealth Poets of Today* and *New Wave Canada*. Ondaatje seems to have understood the politics of publishing early and remains one of the most often anthologized of contemporary Canadian poets. In spite of its auspicious reception, *The Dainty Monsters* is very much a first book – in many poems, overliterary and forced in its expression.

The Man with Seven Toes (1969) was a work of artistic rigor – a dramatic poem of spare, brilliant and often haunting images which was twice its final length in the original draft. Ondaatje has described how the book came about:

There's a series of paintings by Sidney Nolan on this story and I was previously interested in Nolan's Ned Kelly series. I got fascinated by the story of which I only knew the account in the paintings and the quote from Colin MacInnes. That's how it grew. It had to be brief and imagistic because the formal alternative was to write a long graphic introduction explaining the situation, setting, characters and so on.[6]

The Man with Seven Toes was first performed as a dramatic reading for three speakers ("a convict, a lady, and a narrator") by the Gallimaufry Repertory Theatre Company at the 1968 Vancouver Festival; Ken Livingstone was the director. The 1969 Stratford Workshop production was directed by Paul Thompson, whose work with Theatre Passe Muraille was later the inspiration for Ondaatje's film "The Clinton Special." The origins, writing and performances of *The Man with Seven Toes* indicate Ondaatje's fascination with the concrete visual, the eventual move toward film. He has remarked, "I find the editing of a manuscript to be like the editing of a film, that's when you determine the work's shape, rhythmic structures etc."[7]

In 1970, Ondaatje contributed the *Leonard Cohen* volume of McClelland & Stewart's "Canadian Writers" series. The critical monograph is short, 64 pages, and somewhat padded with quotation from Cohen's work, but it has its moments. On a technical level, Ondaatje provides information about Cohen's television interviews and correspondence with his publishers as well as a useful bibliography. On the level of interpretation, Ondaatje eschews a biographical study, or an exploration of the public personality of the writer, and attempts to limit himself to the "pop-sainthood" found in Cohen's work. As might be expected, Ondaatje does not place Cohen's work in relation to an elaborated critical theory but is most to the point when he is analyzing its provocations, passions and sensuality. The visual is especially important, and at a number of points in the monograph, Ondaatje considers the writing in terms of its "cinematic style."

Concerning his next work, and third book of poetry, *The Collected Works of Billy the Kid: Left Handed Poems* (1970), Ondaatje acknowledged that he was

... trying to make the movie I couldn't afford to shoot, in the form of a book. All those B movies in which strange things didn't happen but could and should have happened I explored in the book.[8]

This is perhaps a sufficient explanation of the subtitle. The photograph at the end of the book – of a child in cowboy get-up – is a biographical reference of sorts; asked when he first became interested in Billy the Kid, Ondaatje remarked,

From about the age of seven. Roughly when the last picture in the book (of me in Ceylon in a cowboy outfit) was taken. Then it wasn't specifically Billy the Kid, but *cowboys* that was important. So around 1967 when I began the book the cowboy had germinated. The question that's so often asked – about why I wrote about an American hero – doesn't really interest me cos I hardly knew what an American was when the image of "cowboy" began that germinating process. I was writing about something that had always interested me, something within myself, not out there in a specific country or having some political or sociological meaning. I'm not interested in politics on that public level. The recent fashion of drawing journalistic morals out of literature is I think done by people who don't love literature or who are not capable of allowing its full scope to be seen.[9]

This is an interesting self-description; it indicates that in the aftermath of the appearance of *Billy the Kid,* Ondaatje felt himself to be on the defensive with regard to the significance of his most impressive achievement to that time.[A] His defence of his work makes an important point: literature can never be, nor should it strive to be, only a concrete version of sociological meaning or of political philosophy. But it must be added that literature can never simply be "about something that had always interested me, something within myself" as if a monadic subject is possible and as if it could opt out of social being for such an end. *Billy the Kid* itself offered a more complex tension between subject and culture; later work, especially *Coming Through Slaughter* (1976) and "The Clinton Special" (1974), continued to grapple with the relation of artistic expression to its environment although a statement made in the interval between those works suggests that such development has measured itself against a stubbornly personal and private, even anti-intellectual temper:

I avoid reading books on philosophy, psychology, politics. It's a funny thing, political theses I find impossible to read. I have to be affected emotionally or in a sensual way before something hits me

.....

I can't sit down and read them [Marx or other political theorists] but I can read someone like Tom Wayman and envy that kind of poetry which is about himself and yet also political: he talks about politics, about history as it happens to himself. The book that really affected me in the last year was Marquez's *One Hundred Years of Solitude,* then I read this article on the

A Some of the defensiveness may have come from the demanding editorial process to which the work was subjected at Anansi. In 1977, Ondaatje described his relationship with his editor, Dennis Lee: "As far as I could see, he was the only editor I could trust with the manuscript. As a critic, Dennis is pretty brutal. He doesn't like bullshit. At one point he wants you as a writer to clarify all the intricacies of your work.... You need someone as brutally honest as you would be with yourself – a kind of alter ego or devil's advocate. He made *Billy* more public in a way. It was a very introverted book. He helped me to take it and turn it into a universal rather than just a very personal thing." From: Mark Witten, "The Case of the Midwife Lode," *Books in Canada,* VI (December 1977), 8.

death of Allende and that really knocked me out; it became even more powerful because I had been previously affected by the book.[10]

The dialectic of private vision and environment may have been given a forward direction by Ondaatje's involvement with film-making. Completed in the same year as *Billy the Kid*'s appearance was a 35-minute film documentary on another poet, more self-dramatizing and performance-oriented than Ondaatje, bpNichol. "Sons of Captain Poetry" (1970) was produced with technical assistance from the Queen's University film department and with the collaboration of Robert Fresco and, of course, the subject. The next film, "Carry on Crime and Punishment" (1972), was four minutes in length and not a particularly significant work; Ondaatje seems to have been learning more about the medium. "The Clinton Special" (1974, 70 minutes) – his most important film to date – was shot on very little money in April and August, 1973; it was a documentary of Theatre Passe Muraille's "The Farm Show," dramatizing the life of a farm community near Clinton, Ontario. "The Clinton Special" was not simply a movie version of "The Farm Show" (a lifting-out-of-context which the CBC was to perform) but a critical study of perfor-mance, of the community's response to drama based on their own experiences, of the company's ideas and uncertainties about the experiment, and of the self-characterizations of people from both groups.

In 1973 a dramatization of *Billy the Kid* was produced at Strat-ford (John Wood directed). Ondaatje undertook the dramatic adap-tation of the book himself, and subsequent theatre productions of the work have been generally based on this adaptation although there has been at least one independently developed script. But most theatre presentations have used the Ondaatje script so flexibly that there are almost as many versions of the drama as there have been productions. In accordance with the writer's wishes, there has been no published version of the script. Perhaps Ondaatje does not want the dramatic version to compete in print with the poetry.

The play was produced the next year in New York. Responding (in 1977) to a question about the strong reactions which the play has provoked, Ondaatje said,

With a book you reach the audience you want to reach. In theatre, some-times you have the audience that doesn't know what to expect. If I'd written it originally as a play, it [bad response] would have hurt more. It's like a mirror image, something separate from the book. Each production is very different. But the play continues to cause trouble wherever it goes. Recently, in a New York production of the play, the actor playing Chisum went berserk during a dress rehearsal and tried to kill someone on stage.[11]

A dramatization and a film notwithstanding, the most important 1973 event in the progress of Ondaatje the artist was the appearance of *Rat Jelly,* his third book of poetry to be published with Coach House Press. Ondaatje has maintained a working relationship with Coach House from the publication of his first book to present. The Coach House style of publishing encourages collaboration between publisher and writer on the layout and final appearance of the printed work. Ondaatje has described the collaborative process:

The presentation of the poem is very important to me, and one of the reasons that I work with Coach House so much – and they've designed all my books – is that with Stan Bevington I can talk for several days about design; for example I don't like having to turn over a page in order to finish a poem so that becomes a consideration in the actual design. Certainly with *The Collected Works of Billy the Kid* design was very important. We had to determine the type, the paper design, the paper texture, where the photographs would go, things like the first page on which Billy's photograph doesn't appear. I find it very difficult to write while a finished book is in the process of being printed, cos the printing itself is an art form and I'm deeply involved in it.[12]

His continuing work with Coach House involves editing and advising on manuscripts.

In 1975 Ondaatje demurred from calling his work in progress, *Coming Through Slaughter* (1976), a novel:

Right now I'm working on some prose but if I mention it people say that I'm working on a novel and I'm not. To me the novel is a 100 yard hurdles which you have to plan, prepare etc. And what I'm doing doesn't have a preformed shape. That's why I'm very nervous about what I'm doing right now because it's finding its shape and I've been working on it for 3 or 4 years and there's always a chance it won't work out.[13]

When the work appeared in print, it had been five years in progress, five years of doubt about "the chance it won't work out," involving, along with aesthetic commitments, some serious research into Bolden the jazz musician's life and into the early jazz milieu in New

Orleans. The risks, for a writer who believes that "art is, to a certain extent, deceit" and who states that his first drafts have always seemed "horrendously awful,"[14] must have been great. During the final stages of writing *Coming Through Slaughter,* he published a number of new poems in *The Canadian Forum* under the rubric "Outlaws, Light and Avocadoes" and a critical study of Howard O'Hagan's *Tay John.*

In 1977 Ondaatje published *Personal Fictions: Stories by Munro, Wiebe, Thomas, and Blaise.* Like *The Broken Ark: A Book of Beasts,* a poetry anthology appearing in 1971, *Personal Fictions* had no editorial apparatus, no prefacing remarks. *The Broken Ark* included one of his own poems as well as the work of 22 other writers and the illustrations of Tony Urquhart; in children's book format, it suggested the answer to a need in its gathering of important and accessible Canadian poetry for the joint use of young and adult readers. *The Broken Ark* also bore a direct relation to the side of Ondaatje's work which describes animal life – often, it seems, 'from within' and in its suffering. The bearing of *Personal Fictions* was occult by comparison, though the standard of the selection was high.

Of more moment than the new anthology was the intensification of the published discussion of Ondaatje's work during this year. Reviews of *Coming Through Slaughter* appeared earlier, and in greater number, than reviews had in the case of *Billy the Kid,* and Mark Witten's critical portrait in *Books in Canada* reached an audience which must have been largely unaware of the *Rune* and *Manna* interviews. Scholarly articles from Anne Blott and Sam Solecki suggested growing academic acceptance of the continued significance of Ondaatje's work. Finally, limiting its literary analysis to Leonard Cohen's *Beautiful Losers* and Ondaatje's *Billy the Kid,* Dennis Lee's book-length meditation, *Savage Fields: An Essay in Literature and Cosmology,* was, in Robin Skelton's words,

... calculated to arouse immediate debate, and in tackling two interesting, though flawed, works by two living Canadian writers in a fashion that presumes they deserve and demand sophisticated and rigorous exploration, it may possibly incite others to treat the literature of our country with other than the usual intellectual pusillanimity.[15]

1978 was the year of Ondaatje's first return trip to Sri Lanka, also the year of at least two demanding literary projects – one, the more immediate, preparation of a new and selected poems for 1979 publication, and the other, still some years from completion, the shaping of an autobiographical work with its origins in his Ceylon childhood. By contrast with this ambitious writing, his only publication of 1978, *Elimination Dance*, was a sort of literary home movie. Recalling Nietzsche perhaps ("Living – that is to continually eliminate from ourselves what is about to die"), one might have attempted to make more of this chapbook than it deserved. The list of things to be scourged from the writer (if that's the correct reading of the whip graphic) was genuinely personal in character, without the purpose of satire or, generally, the force of epigram. (Ondaatje's own view of *Elimination Dance* may be indicated by its omission from the biographical blurb of *There's a Trick with a Knife I'm Learning to Do* and from a 1983 selected bibliography which otherwise included all his separately published writings.[16])

In early 1979 *Canadian Forum* published six new Ondaatje poems and in the spring, a collection of selected and new poems appeared, with the title *There's a Trick with a Knife I'm Learning to Do: Poems 1963-1978* (hereafter *Knife,* for want of a more incisive short title). The collection included nothing from *Billy the Kid* or *The Man with Seven Toes* and, surprisingly, only about half the poems from the other two books (18 of 45 poems from *The Dainty Monsters,* 27 of 40 poems from *Rat Jelly*). The presentation of the selected work very much follows the process of revision and editing which Ondaatje described in *Twelve Voices*: "... with a book, what happens usually is that there is a process of editing within the actual individual poem, and also there is a process of structuring the book which is also part of the editing."[17] In the same interview, he explained that revisions of poems after their first publication are limited in scope, where they are necessary at all, because "a lot of the editing has been done *before* the poem goes out." He added, "I tend to keep a poem around for a long time – at least six months or a year – before I send it out."[18] So far as the revision of the selected poems in *Knife* was concerned, there were, apparently, only three poems with changes in language over against the versions in *The Dainty Monsters* and *Rat Jelly*; the changes were quite limited, clarifying the argument rather than recasting it. Several other poems had changes in punctuation, typography or page break.[19] Where the writer's editing of the selected poems had its most obvious results was in the structuring of the book, for the poems in "The Dainty Monsters" and "Rat Jelly" sections of *Knife* don't follow their order in the earlier books. Indeed, "Philoctetes on the Island," from *Rat Jelly,* was placed in association with another Philoctetes poem in "The Dainty Monsters" section, and Ondaatje dropped the suggestive mottoes of the earlier collections in favour of fresh quotations. The nineteen newly collected poems in the "Pig Glass" section of *Knife* revealed the same pattern of limited revision and careful arrangement within the whole. "Light," one of the most ambitious of Ondaatje's shorter poems, underwent a number of changes from its *Canadian Forum* version, but these were matters of detail, giving the poem finish but not much affecting its substance.

There's a Trick with a Knife I'm Learning to Do received the Governor General's Award for poetry in 1979.

The appearance of *The Long Poem Anthology,* also published in 1979 (by Coach House Press), was important for two reasons which need emphasis here. In the first place, as Ondaatje himself pointed out in the book's introduction, an anthology of such work – particularly of poetry from recent years – was long overdue:

> ... it is a form or a 'size' or 'structure' that has been politely ignored by anthologists, schools, and the general reading public. This wouldn't matter if not much was happening with the form, but it seems to me that the most interesting writing being done by poets today can be found within the structure of the long poem.[20]

But if the aggregation of nine long poems of great diversity of technique and direction was an achievement, so was Ondaatje's "missionary work" (to use David Helwig's phrase). Unlike his earlier anthologies, this one had an editorial apparatus, which effectively suggested a range of difficulties in this literature, between readers and writers, between public and private art, between "didactic formal voice" and "naming objects." Following the poems themselves, there was a section of "Statements by the Poets" and then a list of "Recommended Reading." The latter included 77 titles, most this side of 1960. The format of the "Statements" usually involved some comment by the poet on the anthologized work, a short biographical blurb, a bibliography of the poet's writing and of critical comment about this. Finally, the introduction – "What Is in the Pot" – was not only a suggestive commentary but also the sort of explicit statement of Ondaatje's aesthetics which he had rarely offered.

Early 1977 saw yet another well-received production of *Billy the Kid,* this time in Vancouver, performed by the Simon Fraser Group

Theatre and directed by Gordon McCall,[21] and it seemed that the dramatic versions and uses of this work were far from exhausted; but the collaboration between Ondaatje and Theatre Passe Muraille in a stage production of *Coming Through Slaughter* in January, 1980, had no such promising result, to judge from the reviews. Apart from questions about the plausibility of Bolden as a dramatic character, Ondaatje had, for some time, been confronted with an historical Bolden, as delineated in a 1978 study or as speculated about on other grounds.[22] His reaction to this, published in 1980 in the *Twelve Voices* interview:

I have no desire ... to go back and re-write *Billy* or re-investigate Bolden. Just recently there's another book on Bolden that's come out in the States. I have absolutely no desire to read the thing. Even if it gives me all kinds of new material about Bolden, I'm not at all interested in it. For me, Bolden is a character who is important to me only as I knew him. He's there now and I still like him, and now and then I'll see something in the street that I will see the way he saw it.[23]

As with the adaptation of *Billy the Kid*, there has been no published text of the theatre version of *Coming Through Slaughter*.

With another trip to Sri Lanka in 1980, the emphasis again fell upon the writing of *Running in the Family*, a project which linked Ondaatje's creative efforts over the years 1978 through 1982, when the book was published by McClelland and Stewart. There were other projects in this period, of course. Besides those already mentioned, these included: a collaboration with Paul Thompson on a film script of Robert Kroetsch's *Badlands* (an undertaking which, for Ondaatje at least, began in 1976); a number of poems, of which the most significant was the long poem *Tin Roof*, published by the Island Writing Series in 1982; and perhaps another novel, which has only been hinted at in published comment.[24] But *Running in the Family* represented the most significant line of Ondaatje's development over these years. What he said of poetry in the *Twelve Voices* interview was true of his approach to writing generally; the literary work has not been, for Ondaatje, "a total canning of an incident or an event," has not assumed that the writer fully understands "an attitude" before setting to work.[25] *Running in the Family* expanded on those enigmas of personal history which were represented earlier by the childhood photograph in *Billy the Kid*, by "Letters & Other Worlds," by "Light" (dedicated to his mother), with the intention of learning and even with a sense of quest, but not with a 'canned' summing up of the past. There were, of course, physical symbols aplenty of the dissolving family record, but what made the past at some level unknowable was the complexity of human character itself.

Before this complexity in the characters of memory, Ondaatje did not attempt, in a typical autobiographical vein, to recover the past primarily through points of interest offered by his own childhood recollections. With his parents divorced when he was age three or so and with the departure from Ceylon at age 11, these recollections may not have offered the sort of continuity which can be found in other memoirs of earlier years such as Sartre's *Les Mots* and W.H. Hudson's *Far Away and Long Ago*. But also figuring in the choice of experiences through which to write was Ondaatje's own manner as a writer, his reticence before the things that matter deeply to him, the unfolding of discovery through the mediating play of language.

*

A Comment about Methods and Assumptions. To someone surveying contemporary criticism, the range of approaches – structuralism, New Criticism, deconstruction, Marxism, semiotics, archetypal criticism, etc. – may appear to provide means toward convincing command of any subject matter and to obviate the need for much soul-searching. Surely if one critical method doesn't do the trick, another will. Yet, for many, including myself, the plethora of critical nostrums and methodologies is haunted by a curious arbitrariness. As T.H. Adamowski has observed of the new philosophical criticism's linguistic idealism, the slogan of much writing about literature nowadays is "not Berkeley's 'to be is to be perceived' but 'to be is to be in print.'"[26] Indeed, the arbitrariness is not always under wraps; one eminent critic has quite clearly spelled out the authoritarian basis of his work:

I wonder whether some among my hearers, the younger perhaps, may not find what I have said a little cynical and gloomy. I believe that institutions confer value and privilege upon texts, and license modes of interpretation; and that qualification for senior membership of such institutions implies acceptance, not total of course, of this state of affairs. ... It is by recognizing the tacit authority of the institution that we achieve the measure of liberty we have in interpreting. It is a price to pay, but it purchases an incalculable boon; and for my own part I cannot bring myself to say that my conclusions concerning the power of the institution to validate texts and control interpretation are sad ones. They might even be a reason for moderate rejoicing.[27]

Still, if we no longer accept that, say, nuclear reactors are to be considered safe on the basis of institutional validations, it's hard to see how we can confer a higher credibility on the professional teaching of English literature. But institutional authority is certainly not the only source of arbitrariness in contemporary criticism. There are other persuasive authorities with the invisibility of everyday discourse, the hegemonic fabric of a world-view which has usually set the limits to thought in the last two centuries.

Not surprisingly, then, the problems of evaluating literary achievements such as Ondaatje's appeared similar in character to the problem of practical or theoretical argument in ethics as described by Alasdair MacIntyre in *After Virtue: A Study in Moral Theory*. MacIntyre finds the same arbitrariness in present-day moral theory which many of us find in criticism:

The most striking feature of contemporary moral utterance is that so much of it is used to express disagreements; and the most striking feature of the debates in which these disagreements are expressed is their interminable character. I do not mean by this just that such debates go on and on and on – although they do – but also that they apparently can find no terminus. There seems to be no rational way of securing moral agreement in our culture.[28]

Substitute 'critical' for 'moral' in these statements, and they are equally valid. MacIntyre sees this fragmentation of moral vision as stemming from the breakdown of a common religious foundation "for moral discourse and action," the decisive moment in this "catastrophe" being the failure of the Enlightenment project of a philosophical morality. Subsequent moral theory has either accepted this fragmentation as necessary and desirable (Nietzsche being the central example) or provided various unsatisfactory reintegrations, such as utilitarianism and Marxism. The evaluative approaches of moral theory and of criticism have been intertwined since classical philosophy, and the parallels which MacIntyre's work offers to the problematic case of criticism – the historical framework, the disintegration of common standards and of common terms of discourse, the bracketing or masking of evaluations in certain social contexts – suggest why we are awash in mutually exclusive critical vocabularies.

An evaluation of literature seems to require, then, at least three distinct movements, underlying the specific topics of argument. There must be a continuous dialectic involving the vocabulary of discourse, a paranoia about language which is freighted with suggestions of arbitrary structures and approaches. Critical and linguistic terms can be a problem, of course, but psychological language, professional jargon or everyday usage, is possibly a still more frequent difficulty. Secondly, there must be a critique of the historical nature of the writer's discourse, of the criticism itself, and of the period or periods of both; there must be an attempt to understand what Foucault has called the *episteme* of the times in question. Chapter 7, in particular, attempts to place the evaluation of Ondaatje's work within this sort of critique. Thirdly, there must be a movement toward the essence of the work itself; the evaluation of literature must surely be open to discovery, to the sort of excellence which finds us not quite knowing how to explain it – and, in turn, to the rethinking of basic concepts. Each of these movements brings criticism inevitably into a nearer relationship with historical and philosophical concerns.

However, there may be something deceptive about presenting the character of an evaluative approach in this abstract fashion. Although the criticism itself provides a concrete elaboration of the foregoing, it may still be wondered whether my condemnations of amusement art, encapsulated artworks, aesthetic idealism, and taste as a law unto itself are, in fact, only a further symptom of the arbitrariness I've deplored. If they are only matters of logical definition, made up for the occasion, then one consistent set of definitions is as good as another. There is no appeal here from this logical relativism to absolute terms of reference, but the missing piece of the argument is an essentially political view which ties evaluation to what R.D. Laing has called the politics of experience and which may be outlined as follows:

1. "The artistic experience is not generated out of nothing. It presupposes a psychical, or sensuous-emotional, experience."[29]

2. Expression, which is meant here to include not only language but the full repertoire of gesture, is essentially social.

3. "If we are stripped of experience, we are stripped of our deeds; and if our deeds are, so to say, taken out of our hands like toys from the hands of children, we are bereft of our humanity. We cannot be deceived. Men can

and do destroy the humanity of other men, and the condition of this possibility is that we are interdependent."[30]

If this line of thought is valid, then we must be aware of the meaning of the artwork as act – as a choice reflecting some areas of human experience and excluding others, defining a kind of human relating. We must not accept, a priori, that the poet has a privileged relationship to the sheet of paper in his typewriter or to an audience which may be largely detached from the totality of repressed or mundane or liberating expression in society.

*

Acknowledgements. In the course of putting together this study, several works about Ondaatje proved to be especially valuable. Dennis Lee's *Savage Fields* offered a provocative and insightful reading of *Billy the Kid*. Interviews by Sam Solecki and Jon Pearce, published respectively in the magazine *Rune* and in the collection *Twelve Voices,* were – apart from the writer's own works – the most important sources for his views. Also helpful was Mark Witten's critical portrait in *Books in Canada*. Acknowledgement is due the Canadian Filmmakers Distribution Centre (Toronto) for arranging, at short notice, a screening of "Sons of Captain Poetry" and "The Clinton Special." Finally, thanks to Steve Buri for taking an interest in the fate of this project; and to Frank Davey for his criticisms of the manuscript and for his editorial encouragement.

CHAPTER ONE

The Dainty Monsters and the
Problem of Amusement Art

MOST poets probably do not give a great deal of time to considering the chestnut, What is poetry? If the poem works and finds acceptance – better still, if a whole book of poetry works and finds acceptance, then for all practical purposes the question is answered. Nevertheless, it is a good idea for a reader to keep the question in mind, to understand that each volume of poems represents a kind of survival of the fittest, the ones that fell by the wayside representing not failures in view of some timelessly valid conception of poetry upon which everyone should agree but the exclusions dictated by the prevailing codes of the poet's culture. The specific reasons for the abandonment of poems may not, however, be all that easy to discover in the poems themselves. In Ondaatje's case, uncollected poems such as "Pictures from the War," "Little Old Man," and "The Dog Who Loved Bach" pose intriguing but perhaps unanswerable questions about his (or his editors'?) criteria of selection.[1]

Whatever the idealities of criticism in the literary atmosphere of the time, the poet must move, hit and miss, toward a unity of vision which is satisfying to self and to the prospective or actual audience. The surest guide along the way may be anything from a set of technical gimmicks, or the ability to parody already accepted work, to the truth of the poet's own experience; most likely, it is a mixture of patterns for success which the poet follows. This is surely the case with Michael Ondaatje's first book, The Dainty Monsters. This chapter will deal with the way in which this first selection, published when he was 24, hits and misses throughout because Ondaatje had not yet come to terms with the problem of amusement art.

The Dainty Monsters leans more heavily on widely accepted literary standards than much of Ondaatje's later work. Its critical reception gives some idea of how near the poetry was to the literary preconceptions of an audience of professional intellectuals. It was reviewed in Canadian Literature, The Fiddlehead, Queen's

Quarterly, Saturday Night and *University of Toronto Quarterly*. Both the fact that the book rapidly found such an audience – was readily identified as something measuring up to that audience's literary taste – and the somewhat derivative striving for content through 'poetic' technical means raise the question of whether *The Dainty Monsters* is dominated by amusement values as opposed to significant art values.

In characterizing this distinction between amusement art (Collingwood's phrase) and significant art, it is possible to give both physiological and phenomenological criteria.[A]

In physiological terms, amusement art is pleasurably stimulating but not so stimulating that it is problematic. An artwork with a great deal of novelty (where *novelty* refers not to avant-gardist tendencies but to all possible challenges to understanding) is not immediately pleasing, or not entirely so, although with persistence it may give pleasure as well as evoke other responses. As Tibor Scitovsky explains in *The Joyless Economy,*

Novelty creates a problem, and its enjoyment comes from the resolution of the problem. In order to enjoy information, I must understand it and make it my own; by doing so I reduce and, ultimately, eliminate its subjective novelty by incorporating it into the already familiar.[2]

It is obvious that a not-too-strenuous imaginative exercise in absorbing a poem's familiar content (form, assertion, argument, characterization of experience) may mean a response very similar in kind to the enjoyment of works which are readily identifiable as amusement art. Whether the poem or poetry in question involves literary references may or may not be relevant. Such references may make the poetry more difficult for an audience who are not in the know; but for the cognoscenti, they are often not at all puzzling.

Pleasure, as schematized by Scitovsky on the basis of physiologi-

---

A *Phenomenological* and other forms of the word, when not used to refer to a movement in the history of ideas, refer, in a general way, to an evaluative examination of the structure of experience. This usage is not meant to include automatic reference to a naturalistic metaphysical grounding of the sciences or to an existential psychology, either of which would be linked to the modernist perspective described in Chapter 7. Rather, as the "Introduction" suggests, it has to do with orientation of argument within a politics of experience – a political dimension of the phenomenological movement emerging in the works of Sartre and Merleau-Ponty – and with the corresponding necessity of defining and redefining experience within a developing political perspective.

cal psychology, is either arousal reduction (the securing of comfort following a level of arousal that is too high) or increasing arousal from a low level of stimulation (boredom) to an optimum state of stimulated comfort. Extrapolating from Scitovsky's discussion of these quite different kinds of satisfaction, I want to argue that reading necessarily involves some level of imaginative construction and that our pleasure in this construction flows from either of the abovementioned sources – either from arousal reduction or from a stimulated comfort somewhere just above boredom.

One obvious and important difference between reading a poem or a novel and seeing a film is that in doing the former, we are not immediately perceiving the thing which the artwork is about, and, should we stop the task of imaginative construction and perhaps see only words on the page, we lose contact with the subject. Whether or not we make an effort to fully understand film on its most significant level, to some extent meanings are already there in perception and offer a continuity of their own, which, if it is not what the filmmaker intended us to see, nevertheless sustains our attention. By contrast with film and television, reading involves, of necessity, a higher level of arousal,[3] and the primary means of reducing the degree of this requirement are habitual reading and a high level of redundancy in what is read.

In Scitovsky's terms, amusement art is characterized by a high level of redundancy and mildly stimulating novelty which does not go beyond the optimum level of arousal required to cope with boredom without adding a further level of discomfort. Such art is found to be pleasing rather than interesting.[4] It may seem that such a description could not apply to literary works; surely, the level of novelty in literary works precludes associating them with comfort rather than with pleasure! But literature which appeals to a literary audience is making a case for those who have developed habitual reading skills of great variety. For such an audience, the level of arousal required by a literary work may not be much beyond the optimum stimulation required for contrast with boredom. If the problematic character of the work is minimized or even directed into recognizable forms which can be accepted as a literary *result,* there need not be anything particularly uncomfortable or strained about the reception of a work which ostensibly includes a good deal of novelty.

When we consider novelty in literature, we have to think in terms of the tremendous range of devices, images and thought which the literary audience might already be prepared to accept in artwork. What would seem intensely novel to a reader with no 'literary background' is often mainstream stuff to the cognoscenti. True, *novelty* is a somewhat misleading term for what cuts closest to the bone in literature since discovery within our own experiences doesn't so much reveal something new as insist on the truth of something which everyday responses cover up. Our capacity to handle this kind of 'novelty' is measured by our capacity to imagine: other selves, other relations, other societies. If imagination retreats from this, we may very well find the same thought startling, and embarrassing, even a second or third time around.

The physiological criteria for the analysis of amusement art permit us to approach the reception of a particular artwork only in the most general way; the terms of this analysis – *arousal, pleasure, sedate stimulation, novelty,* etc. – belong themselves to a generalized view of the problem and would not necessarily be as useful in considering reception in its totality. To give critical usefulness to the concept of amusement art, it is necessary, as well, to consider it phenomenologically.

R.G. Collingwood's definition of amusement art is a good starting point:

If an artifact is designed to stimulate a certain emotion, and if this emotion is intended not for discharge into the occupations of ordinary life, but for enjoyment as something of value in itself, the function of the artifact is to amuse or entertain.[5]

Collingwood argues that "In order that an emotion may be discharged without affecting practical life, a make-believe situation must be created in which to discharge it."[6] How is it possible for a literary work to function as "make-believe"?

The possibility arises, as Collingwood points out, when the literary work belongs to a hedonistic theory of art. If the ground of the real has been co-opted by instrumentalist description, it is understandable that literary works should be considered as offering a kind of ornamental or secondhand reality to be appreciated for its own sake. And the hazard of such appreciation and of the literature which evokes it is that, encapsulated on its own terms, the artwork becomes "make-believe." If the materials of art can be entirely detached from mundane experience (which, ideologically, demands an instrumental explanation), they may paradoxically reappear as an art-science or an art-game.

It is possible to accept the problem of the encapsulated artwork and yet to insist that the artwork should be entertaining. Collingwood's response to this is: "... even if the function of art is to give 'delight' (as many good artists have said), still this delight is not pleasure in general but pleasure of a particular kind." He points out that, in providing amusement, the artwork ceases to be a work of art proper but is "simply a means to an end," having no value in itself.[7] The pleasure it gives is, therefore, bounded in a particular way and quite distinct from the pleasure we take in something which touches our lives in a significant way.

Thus, if a poem suggests, in reception, that it is offering a self-contained experience, it is necessary to consider whether there is not, fundamentally, a confusion between the pleasing use of varied technical means to create a word-artifact and the more fundamental experience we associate with significant art. It is quite legitimate to question, if amusement art and significant works appear together in the same volume, as they do in *The Dainty Monsters,* whether the writer has consistent objectives in expression.

Since whether a poem is identifiable as amusement art is contingent, to some extent, on the reader's background, I will begin with reasonably clear-cut examples to indicate the distinction between amusement art and significant art in *The Dainty Monsters.* Consider the poem "Application for a Driving License," which can be quoted here in full:

Two birds loved
in a flurry of red feathers
like a burst cottonball,
continuing while I drove over them.

I am a good driver, nothing shocks me.

In spite of the brevity, this is a powerful work. The first four lines not only establish a situation but offer a calculating description by contrast with the surprise and horror expected of this experience. The phrase "nothing shocks me" extends this ambiguity still further, by apparently referring to the sexuality of the birds as well as to the cool of the driver, and because of the tension between our expectations and the sensibility actually expressed, the questions arise: Why does nothing shock the driver? Why is the driver a *good* driver? As the possible extensions of the poem suggest themselves, it becomes clear that the poem is not, expressively, a self-contained artifact and that it touches on experiences which do not offer ready-made lines of resolution and categorization. It is, in other words, *significant* in a rigorous sense because it signifies more than itself or, put another way, meaning is not subordinated to, or reducible to, a technical demonstration. The technical means of the poem, in fact, reinforce its signifying character. The only simile intensifies the first lines without obstructing the emphasis; the leaps of thought with their ambiguity and irony do not suggest a paraphrasing of conventional reality description. We are not reminded that this is something which 'fits in' with what a sociologist or psychologist said the other day.

"The Sows" is cleverly worked up amusement art. Almost every line offers a creative moment of syntax and / or metaphor which must be puzzled out (without much effort) and appreciated as technical resource. But the creative moments never add up to more than rambling (if brilliant) description:

So chinless duchesses
sniff out the day
gauging their loves with a seasoned eye.
On spread thighs, and immobile,
they categorize the flux around them,
watching the rain melting the dust,
or the sun
fingersnapping out the dying summer.
(*DM* 15)

Nothing is unresolved; we do not require an intuition reaching beyond the poem because no questions of any significance have been broached. To Ondaatje's credit, there is no lunge after meaning, no technical obfuscation of limited content; other poets have done worse in trivial writing. And the poem is essentially trivial since it is working up an insignificant subject matter for the technical uses of the grammatical, rhetorical and logical functions of language. The static nature of these functions, dissociated from the organic necessity of imagination and experience, helps to explain why, for all the imagery, "The Sows" has the forced consecutiveness of a piece of journalistic or factual description.

More complex instances of the predominance of amusement art

values are a number of the narrative poems in the "Troy Town" section of the book. In this section Ondaatje leans most heavily on
literary 'tradition' and a fashionable critical conception of myth. The
aestheticism of the writing relies on a critical idealism to guarantee
significance while the writer's experience, insofar as it is even necessary, gives itself up to the artwork. In these narratives of *The Dainty
Monsters* there is a kind of stereotyping of the artwork from which
Ondaatje does not decisively emerge until *The Collected Works of
Billy the Kid.*

The poem "O Troy's Down: Helen's Song" is a good example of
sophisticated amusement art – a self-contained aesthetic exercise
with little or no significance. The reader may find it mildly stimulating to place the narration against the background of the Trojan War,
to identify Helen's relatives in this background and to see if the emotions in the poem seem to fit the story. Once this is accomplished, the
reader can only accept the poem's structure of feeling as satisfactory
within the artwork; there is no other level suggesting that the poem is
an urgent translation of some contemporary experience. (That probably wouldn't have succeeded either.) At the end of the poem there is
simply nothing more. The poem might signify something if the story
of Troy had intrinsic literary value and if complex emotions were
universals; but the meaning of Troy must be developed anew in any
work which takes up that subject matter and the emotions of the
poem are necessarily contemporary even if they lack real reference.
Because the poem's meanings are encapsulated, there is an arbitrariness of technique similar in character to that of "The Sows." It is possible to admire the invention, but the only unity – Helen interpreted –
is the static sum of the emotional states referred to it, again an essentially trivial construction. Whether the poem works depends on
whether the reader is willing to make-believe, in an exercise of reading skills, that the character so constructed could exist (or perhaps
that such works reflect the essence of literature).

While, in length and in the scope of what is attempted, "Peter" is
the most ambitious writing in *The Dainty Monsters*, it is also troub-
led by the amusement art syndrome. The poem moves through the
capture of a wild child (sections I and II) and his torment and discipline by villagers and court (sections III and IV) to his development as
an artist (sections V and VI) and, finally, his rape of Tara (section VII).
Each of these moments in the poem would, superficially, appear to
have a complexity and significance of content which would place it

beyond the encapsulated experience of amusement art. And yet, if the poem is carefully examined for significant reference – structures of meaning transcending the poem itself, the matter is not so clear. The poem itself gives no sufficient indication of historical time, place, or culture. "Villagers" and "court" are not further elaborated upon. We are apparently being presented with "a myth" – something presumed not to require this kind of qualification. But the action of the poem makes clear just how mistaken this view of myth's nature is:

They snared him in evening light,
his body a pendulum
between the walls of the yard,
rearing from shrinking flashes of steel
until they, with a new science,
stretched his heels and limbs,
scarred through the back of his knees
leaving his veins unpinned,
and him singing in the evening air. (*DM* 72)

The imagery of cruelty has some shock value, perhaps, but only a confused reality because the "villagers" are anonymous, or, to be more exact, they do not exist, except in the label. The phrase "with a new science" echoes the first line of another poem in the book, "Prometheus, with Wings": "They splayed him scientifically on the rock / ..." In both instances, the language seems to refer to a rationalism or instrumentalism which does not, in fact, emerge from the poetry.

With its narrative unity bound up with a single character, perhaps "Peter" could have succeeded in spite of the abstraction of time and place if the character itself were presented with a certain plausibility. But it is precisely in characterization that the contradictions at work in the poem become most glaring. In the first year after capture, Peter's tongue is cut out:

There followed months of silence,
then the eventual grunting;
he began to speak with the air of his body,
torturing breath into tones; it was despicable,
they had made a dead animal of his throat.

He was little more than a marred stone,
a baited gargoyle, escaped
from the fountain in the courtyard:
his throat swollen like an arm muscle,
his walk stuttered with limp, his knees straight,
his feet arcing like a compass. (*DM* 73)

Even before losing his tongue, Peter's "words were growls, meaning-less" to his captors. From this state, in which language is reduced to "torturing breath into tones," "scowls and obscenities," and "sud-den grins," Peter emerges as an artist or, rather, The Artist:

All this while Peter formed violent beauty.
He carved death on chalices,
made spoons of yawning golden fishes;
forks stemmed from the tongues of reptiles,
candle holders bent like the ribs of men.

He made fragments of people: breasts
in the midst of a girl's stride,
a head burrowed in love,
an arm swimming – fingers heaved
to nose barricades of water. (*DM* 75)

The poem gives no insight into how the sophistication of such an artist could be found in a brutalized human being who is "the court monster"; it simply and incorrectly assumes that this could be the case or, perhaps, that it doesn't matter, especially in the realm of 'myth.' But the 'myth' of the artist in "Peter" is undercut completely by the abstraction from time and place and by the improbability of Peter's development. Nor is the poem redeemed, finally, by the plau-sibility of the rape. It is plausible that an isolated and brutalized per-son might turn against, even do violence to, the one who offered kindness or attempted to help. To the extent that "Peter" involves us in the emotions of such a situation, it rises above amusement art. Yet the final section must be related to what went before. The rape then shares the unreality of the poem's lack of significant reference and the shortcomings of its 'myth' of the artist.

Considering only the "Troy Town" poems, one might feel that the solution to the amusement art syndrome would be for the poet to concern himself with things closer to home. However, a good number of poems in the "Over the Garden Wall" portion of the book

are closer to home, and they are not of any profounder significance.
Consider the description of a house at night in "The Republic":

Too much reason in its element
passions crack the mask in dreams.
While we sleep
the plants in frenzy heave floors apart,
lust with common daisies,
feel rain,
fling their noble bodies, release a fart.
The clock alone, rigid and superior,
swaggers in the hall.

At dawn gardenias revitalize
and meet the morning with decorum. (*DM* 20)

The idea which structures the poem is hardly new — that is, the opposition between reason and passion, order and disorder. The description is active, possesses a certain 'magical realism.' But there is no
tension in the poem; it is clearly enjoyable, self-sufficient, encapsulated — amusement art. Surprisingly, even the poems which express
intimacy are similarly bounded. The personal remains the personal
as, for example, in " 'Lovely the Country of Peacocks' ":

My daughter cackling in defiance
voices mystic yells like a snake charmer,
a fulica in the afternoon.

Her buddhist stomach is boasted,
....
she struggles for tender goals:
her mother's hair,
the crumpled paper.
.....
Looking on
we wear sentimentality like a curse.

Her body bears, inside the changing flesh,
rivers of collected suns,
jungles of force, coloured birds
and laziness. (*DM* 41)

Again, there is that sense in the description of a forced consecutiveness. Do "rivers of collected suns" and "jungles of force" finally

move us beyond the poem? Perhaps they do, in a general and inconclusive way. Nothing else does. The clue to the amusement art of *The Dainty Monsters* might be in that line "we wear sentimentality like a curse." A young poet's commitment to writing about the world is tempered by the realization that the world has a way of contradicting young poets. In the critical atmosphere of the Sixties there were technical means in abundance to avoid this painful encounter: 'objective correlative,' 'archetype,' 'myth,' debased 'surrealism,' etc.

Ondaatje's early long narrative poems, "Peter" and *The Man with Seven Toes,* disclose the aestheticism of the university, forcing a conformity to its ideal values and promoting literary artifacts of its hesitancies and prejudices. Narrative itself extends meanings in directions which cannot be strictly controlled in a long poem; the artwork outruns the artist, emphases emerge that may very well be understood differently in reception than they were in the working out of the artist's intention. I have already shown how "Peter" founders on an implausibility and how the final section of the poem at least approaches a level of significance quite distinct from what precedes it. In *The Collected Works of Billy the Kid,* Ondaatje found another dimension for imagination and a way out of the aestheticist straitjacket.

One of the important changes over Ondaatje's writing from *The Dainty Monsters* to *Coming Through Slaughter* is a developing view of the relation between what might be called entertainment values and the essential seriousness of art. In an interview shortly after the publication of *Billy the Kid,* he said, "I find that idea that art should not forget to be entertainment really important,"[8] one implication being that art is more. A central conflict for Buddy Bolden as jazz artist (*Coming Through Slaughter*) involves his rejection of amusement art, art which is "just a utensil." Bolden has learned a different art from his teachers:

So Galloway taught me not craft but to play a mood of sound I would recognize and remember. Every note new and raw and chance. Never repeated. His mouth also moving and trying to mime the sound but never able to for his brain had lost control of his fingers.[9]

Robichaux the entertainer is for a moment appealing when Bolden has reached a point of mere existence, can no longer (in one of Ondaatje's skilful images) decipher two hours of radio "about a crisis":

Did you ever meet Robichaux? I never did. I loathed everything he stood for. He dominated his audiences. He put his emotions into patterns which a listening crowd had to follow. My enjoyment tonight was because I wanted something that was just a utensil. Had a bath, washed my hair, and wanted the same sort of clarity and open-headedness. But I don't believe it for a second.[10]

The last statement has particular significance for Ondaatje's own development; in the later books, *Rat Jelly, Billy the Kid, Coming Through Slaughter,* there is an explicit concern with art as 'deceit' or 'lying.' While he concedes that "There's a great deal of lying in poetry, by necessity," he also wants an "emotional or psychological rightness"[11] in his work. Other writers would perhaps find those adjectives too limited to describe the revelation or projection of the range of experience; *emotional* and *psychological* seem to refer to the problematic subjectivity permitted to artistic expression by a world in which truth is depersonalized. Nevertheless, Ondaatje's direction for his work clearly means something other than, and more significant than, amusement art. We can understand what he is saying about entertainment values in this context. Entertainment values – as opposed to amusement values – need not be encapsulated, irrelevant, trivial. The example of a significant entertainment which Ondaatje himself gave in the *Rune* interview is the film "Once upon a Time in the West":

... emotionally I like that film's expansiveness and I find it a very moving film in the way it deals with the destruction of social violence by the violence of outsiders – something that interests me. ... It also contains the whole history of the western: there's a scene where just before the family is shot all the birds fly off which Leone has literally taken from John Ford's *The Searchers*; the shooting through the boot is from a Gene Autry film and so on.[12]

Entertainment is a word which suggests many levels of fascination with the artwork, and the levels indicated in the interview and in much of his work clearly go beyond amusement, the consumption of art. They are levels of significance which speak to our essential relations to the world.

CHAPTER TWO

The Man With Seven Toes: Logical Interrogation and Context in Reception

MOST readers, beginning from the beginning, would probably have some difficulty with *The Man with Seven Toes*, not because the phrasing of the poetry is cryptic (it isn't) but because the first pages of the poem do not offer a sufficient context for the possibilities of the language. Part of the difficulty may be explained away by the fact that the poem was written for a dramatic reading, and, if there are no labels in the book to identify the dramatic voices, there is at least a program note at the end of the poem to identify the source of the narrative. The note is taken from Colin MacInnes; to avoid a paraphrase of the poem, I give it in full:

Mrs Fraser was a Scottish lady who was shipwrecked on what is now Fraser Island, off the Queensland Coast. She lived for 6 months among the aborigines, rapidly losing her clothes, until she was discovered by one Bracefell, a deserting convict who himself had hidden for 10 years among the primitive Australians. The lady asked the criminal to restore her to civilization, which he agreed to do if she would promise to intercede for his free pardon from the Governor. The bargain was sealed, and the couple set off inland.

At first sight of European settlement, Mrs Fraser rounded on her benefactor and threatened to deliver him up to justice if he did not immediately decamp. Bracefell returned disillusioned to the hospitable bush, and Mrs. Fraser's adventures aroused such admiring interest that on her return to Europe she was able to exhibit herself at 6d a showing in Hyde Park.

The poem does not follow this storyline too closely. The protagonist is inadvertently left in the desert by a train rather than shipwrecked. The poem ends abruptly with her return to civilization ("Potter" the convict drops out of sight) and with a song which alludes to her performances as a speaker on the subject of her adventures:

The people drank the silver wine
they ate the meals that came in pans

And after eating watched a lady
singing with her throat and hands (*MWST* 42)

The dramatic intent of the poem does not fully explain the paring
down of exposition and the minimalist approach to language, which
require a program note.

   One effect of stripping the poetry to 'essentials' is to de-emphasize
narrative voice and to compel an imaginative effort to comprehend
the personae, thereby enhancing, sometimes with great vividness,
the dramatic presence of gesture. Working against this, however, is
the carefully imposed unity of style. At times, it detracts from the
imaginative connections which ask to be made. Take for example the
first segment of the poem:

She moved to the doorless steps
where wind could beat her knees.
When they stopped for water she got off
sat by the rails on the wrist thick stones.

The train shuddered, then wheeled away from her.
She was too tired even to call.
Though, come back, she murmured to herself. (9)

Phrases such as "where wind could beat her knees" and "wrist thick
stones" do not suggest the sensibility or even the immediate experience of the Mrs. Fraser character so much as they indicate a conventional narrator and the 'heightened' poetic language itself. (On the
other hand, the phrase "wheeled away" is not a concise suggestion of
the pulling out of the train but can be construed as the protagonist's
afterimage, a kind of image-sum in the immediate recollection of the
train's departure. As such, the phrase introduces the phenomenal
suggestiveness of the next two lines.)

   To the poet who considers that historical narrative in prose must
develop, conventionally, along lines akin to classical realism and
that poetry, by contrast, must be condensed and imagistic, exposition is anathema, so much dull stage direction for the action to
follow and a serious obstacle to the intensification of language in
reception which the poet cultivates as an ideal. Ondaatje's solution
to the narrative problem in *The Man with Seven Toes* was to truncate
exposition, wherever it became necessary to have it, and to rely on a
program note to give background and to tie up certain loose ends.
Setting is, therefore, ambiguous throughout the poem since it is produced both from the poet's mannered avoidance of classical narra-

tive and from his insight into the phenomenal links of action he portrays. The minimalist exposition does, however, enhance at times the dramatic voices of the poem and suggests, by its very combination of vividness and incompleteness, the shock, exhaustion and suffering of the protagonist.

Given the limitations of reference in the poem, the poem-in-its-contexts, which is the only comprehensible poem, persistently confronts the reader with discontinuities at a number of semantic levels, requiring a kind of response which I'll call *logical interrogation* – a kind of response which is bracketed within, or subordinated to, the overall process of imaginative construction. Logical interrogation does not imply the necessity of absolute (ideal) comprehension of the work. There are differences in the number of unknowns which different readers will accept or pass over in the process of finding meaning; and there are differences in the desired comprehension of the same reader from reading to reading. It is useful to consider the obstacles to the logical interrogation of meaning in parallel with the obstacles to the development of new theory in the sciences. Given a certain level of experience in literary techniques or the methods of a science, it is always possible for the reader or scientific worker to pick up the structural or theoretical clues to a likely solution of a particular problem – that is, to identify the clues readily with an acceptable existing structure of thought and thereby to assume that the significance of the matter at hand is settled. The congruency between what is observed and the prior theoretical framework for observation need not in fact be very great for the process of interrogation to take this course. Writers have, naturally, the option of creating works which seem to challenge the major props of their readers' expectations of literature. But their works, just as incongruent natural phenomena, may be minimized or subsumed in arbitrary ways for the sake of the conservation of an established view. It is, therefore, no small task for the writer to engage an audience in the construction of new meanings and a different order of thought. Some of the problems of logical interrogation which readers of *The Man with Seven Toes* must resolve are:

1. *The identity of narrative voice.* As, for example, in the segment:

Lost my knife. Threw the thing at a dog
and it ran away, the blade in its head.
Sometimes I don't believe what's going on. (27)

In this passage, the "I" is identified by way of the storyline given at the back, by the 'masculine' image and possession of the knife, by contrast with the narrator of the previous segment and by a process of elimination. (Could it be anyone but Potter the convict?) The process of identification involves a logical construction which must precede a fully satisfactory reading.

2. *The problem of mediation.* Contemporary poetry has an uneasy relationship with stereotypes of historical, sociological or non-fiction presentation. In the case of *The Man with Seven Toes,* the reader must, for example, decide not only whether the poem attempts to reconstruct a historical sensibility but also what relationship a historical event has to the imaginative scope and purposes of the writing. Even if the writer rejects the stereotypes of social 'data,' the work may be written around this territory as if the truth of such stereotypes and the artwork have to do with mutually exclusive subject matters. A negative critical concept which is freighted with this problem is *mediation.* The development of this concept comes from the view, characterized by Raymond Williams, that "We should not expect to find (or always to find) directly 'reflected' social realities in art...." In the artwork,

... the social realities are 'projected' or 'disguised,' and to recover them is a process of working back through the mediation to their original forms. ... If we remove the elements of mediation, an area of reality, and then also of the ideological elements which distorted its perception or which determined its presentation, will become clear.[1]

But mediation, in this approach, typically presupposes that the social reality which is mediated is the objective discovery of scientific methods of observation, experiment and theory development and that, as such, its truth is historically more fundamental than the 'truth' of the artwork (if by contrast with such a formidable explanation the artwork can even be characterized as communicating truth). What happens to produce this view is that the historical conditions of scientific work or logical system-making are ignored, or suppressed as unimportant, in favour of a methodological ideal and ideological purity. Scientific ideology may so completely dominate our understanding of observation and theory that even in cases where divergent theories claim the same subject matter, we ignore their incommensurability and proceed on the assumption that there is a common ground. In any case, we may be led to ignore or minimize the role of professional groups, class influences, economic pressures and political considerations in the development of research programs in the sciences.

It is a rare contemporary work which does not present, at least implicitly, some version of the problem of mediation. Most contemporary Canadian poetry is either written around the domain of an objective or factual social reality or self-consciously mediates such a reality or (most interesting of all) incorporates stereotyped social reality ironically. There is no reason for the literary work to concede a greater measure of reality to scientific ideology or to critical principles which attempt to incorporate that ideology in the rationalization and mystification of literature – if only because the basis of both the sciences and literature is in a historical and particular human condition. As Paul Feyerabend states, in a simple and unanswerable argument for the incommensurability of theories in the sciences,

... incommensurability has an analogue in the field of perception and ... is part of the history of perception. ... the development of perception and thought in the individual passes through stages which are mutually incommensurable.[2]

What, then, becomes of the problem of mediation in *The Man with Seven Toes*? The poem avoids sociological interpretation of the dramatic personae, anthropological reference to the aborigines, all but inspirational contact with the historical event of Mrs. Fraser's shipwreck. These exclusions are not incidental or accidental. The fact that Ondaatje skirted an historical or *interpretive* line of thought only emphasizes its absence. In trying to resolve the significance of this paradox in this case, it is rather useless to insist that, in spite of its 'subjective idealism,' Ondaatje's poetry betrays such-and-such characteristics of factually hygienic reality. A more effective analytical approach involves a further moment in logical interrogation:

3. *The epistemic or truth-value condition of the imaginative construction of meaning.* Once it is clear that in *The Man with Seven Toes,* Ondaatje looks to an experience which is separate from and perhaps more fundamental than a factual (objective historical and / or scientific) accounting of reality, the question arises, How can this expression of the poet's experience in terms of a subject matter apparently so remote from it be less artificial than, say, an

abstraction of social theory? Such a question leads to a consideration of the truth-value precondition of the imaginative construction of meaning from text or performance.

Schiller accurately described the problem of artificial treatment of subject matter in literature:

Taste must never forget that it carries out an order emanating elsewhere, and that it is not its own affairs it is treating of. All of its parts must be limited to place our minds in a condition favorable to knowledge; over all that concerns knowledge itself it has no right to any authority. For it exceeds its mission, it betrays it, it disfigures the object that it ought faithfully to transmit, it lays claim to authority out of its proper province; if it tries to carry out there, too, *its own* law, which is nothing but that of pleasing the imagination and making itself agreeable to the intuitive faculties; if it applies this law not only to the *operation,* but also to the *matter* itself; if it follows this rule not only to arrange the materials but to choose them.

.....

In general it is unsafe to give to the aesthetical sense all its culture before having exercised the understanding as the pure thinking faculty, and before having enriched the head with conceptions; for as taste always looks at the carrying out and not at the basis of things, wherever it becomes the only arbiter, there is an end of the essential difference between things. Men become indifferent to reality, and they finish by giving value to form and appearance only.[3]

With due allowance for Schiller's faculty psychology and handling of imagination,[B] this accurately sets out the conditions on which the truth-value of a literary work may be bracketed or subordinated to aestheticism. This account of taste parallels, in part, the objections to amusement art in the previous chapter. *The Man with Seven Toes* is

B   For some comment on Schiller's view of imagination, see pp. 65-67. The basis of faculty psychology was implicit in the medieval hypostatizing of vices and virtues (and of other typifications of human activity), but faculty psychology itself emerged in the seventeenth and eighteenth centuries as a strategy for the comprehensive description of the *natural* order of mind. The categorization of experience by mental faculties provided a metaphysical basis both for the naturing of mind in parallel with other discoveries of natural law and for the support of traditional ethical and religious views. Thus, by Schiller's time, faculty psychology already stood in contrast to a thoroughgoing materialism (partly based on new discoveries in medicine and physiology) and to the beginnings of an experimental psychology with utilitarian and instrumentalist implications. Nevertheless, phrenology, with a wide appeal but an increasingly suspect metaphysical basis, continued to sustain the influence of faculty psychology through the first half of the nineteenth century.

dominated by aestheticism, a taste which is a law unto itself. Ondaatje has maintained a careful line of division between the poem's reality and our own. But I want to contend, at a later stage in the discussion, that conflicting truth-values are at work in the poem, that the imposed law of taste does not have the field all to itself.

*

The foregoing kinds of logical interrogation in an imaginative construction of *The Man with Seven Toes* are not the only ones required for a satisfying reading of the work. Although there is a great range in what different readers require by way of coherence and comprehension in the case of any particular work, I think most readers of this poem would make contact with logical discontinuities roughly at the points indicated even if some readers would not pursue an explanation very far. Some problems of logical interrogation, such as the identity of the narrator, syntactic innovation, some metaphors, are set by the writer in roughly the terms in which they are received. Other problems of this kind, such as coherence of characterization and secondary levels of meaning, may be quite unplanned. In any case, the problems of logical interrogation interrupt the routine flow of imaginative construction and throw readers back upon their resources. The most likely solution to a problem which involves the reconciliation of contraries is to locate them in a context which includes them both. This process should not be considered an unnecessary obstacle which the writer throws in the reader's way; it is, instead, one of the primary means by which the writer indicates (in some cases, finds) that there is something more in the work than a cliché of expression.

A convenient starting point for considering context is offered by the bifurcation of contexts in literary works into the categories: 1) contexts of production and 2) contexts of reception.

In a phenomenological, structural or historical criticism, production and reception contexts are inseparable from the 'poem itself,' or, rather, the 'poem itself,' without such contexts, does not exist. Where reception is concerned, context is a necessity in the process by which the text or utterance of a poem becomes a meaningful thing. *The Man with Seven Toes* would seem to defy contextual analysis since the writer has reduced the narrative to a 'mythic' construction which even lacks appropriate geographical and historical reference points. Notwithstanding the occasional reviewer who believed that the Mrs. Fraser character represented a Victorian sensibility, the language of the different narrative voices is of limited credibility as historical characterization. It is, however, precisely the lack of this conventional sense of context which suggests the aestheticism which is the first clue to grasping the intended direction and scope of the work. (How a theatre audience would have responded is not easy to guess; in a script for dramatic voices, it would seem necessary to offer an audience the Colin MacInnes quotation at the beginning of the performance.) Even with its encapsulated meanings, then, *The Man with Seven Toes* requires, in the reading process, a contextual analysis which reckons with the writer's choices in supplying some reference points for meaning and in omitting others.

Ondaatje's choices of such reference points have been dictated by, among other things, what he feels is appropriate to poetry or to a poetic language and what he believes the reader must have to understand or puzzle out the narrative and argument of the work (for a theatre company, the possible structures of presentation of the work). Not all the clues necessary for establishing contexts of the work are conscious choices of the writer. In many works of literature, we are aware of contradictions between the reality which a writer attempts to establish and a countervailing meaning which undercuts the writer's plan.

A further caveat in contextual analysis is that the distinction between production- and reception-contexts is only a tool for sorting out confusions. As such, it can be misapplied and create some confusions of its own. Some production-contexts are almost inevitably filtered through the contexts of reception. For example, although it's true that there can be in interpretation an overly speculative approach to the writer's intentions, it is also true that reading a literary work requires the ascription of intentions to whatever personae or characterizing gestures (including those of the writer) happen to emerge from the language. This is not some sort of universal prejudice in the reading of literature. It is simply the result of the reflexive nature of language. Before language can be a dead letter or at least a dismembered and classified lexis, it must be the means by which, continuously, the being of a culture is sustained and re-created anew. We cannot read or listen to poetry without reflexively ascribing intentions and moods which open to us the situation and meaning of of the work, which offer us a kind of participation in these things through the medium of our social existence, language.

Although, clearly, consideration of what a writer intended in a work will be filtered through reception-contexts, not every significant production-context is entirely or largely dependent on response to the poem itself. Quite apart from questions of reception, it is possible to consider the writer's social class and education, the level of prestige and the class character of literature in the writer's culture, and that culture's publishing industry and / or opportunities for presentation of works. None of these considerations may change the response to a particular literary work; however, they can frequently make more comprehensible the choices which determined the existence of the work but which may be largely invisible in the final result.

Coming back to *The Man with Seven Toes*, I think the interpretive problematic of the work is, generally, somewhat as follows:

The reader finds the work not readily accessible, even if there are many immediate and telling images and the reader is offered a kind of explanation of the work, the Colin MacInnes quote – that is, a clue to the storyline and its historical precedent. But, finally, this is not a wholly satisfactory statement upon which to base a reading. It suffers from all those drawbacks and ambiguities of purpose associated in music history with program notes to the concert work. Does the program tell us how we are to respond to the work? But the feeling of the poem is much different from that of the historical anecdote. Does the program, then, help us to situate the work in our experience? Of course, the poem remains vaguely situated with respect to historical and geographical contexts. Does the program tell us what the story is really about? Only in an oblique way, it turns out. To get at the relation between the anecdote and the poem, it is necessary to consider, in fact, the whole range of contextual questions which arise in reading.[4]

The references which seem to underpin the poem and to offer important clues for a coherent reading of it have a common, striking characteristic; they are opposites to what we might conceive of as Ondaatje's own experience:

Focus of Reference	Writer's Experience	Poem's World
sex	man	protagonist = woman
setting	urban	desert
society	Canadian	aboriginal / Australian
time	1960s	1830s

The terms of opposition are so comprehensive that they raise questions 1) about the extent to which the work might be a denial of the writer's situation, 2) about the character of the language which functions as go-between for the oppositions, and 3) about the success of the evocation (for how was it possible for the writer to evoke an apparently other world with such minimal narrative detail?).

1. On the first point, it might be said that much of Ondaatje's literary work to date denies any frame which would be readily recognized as a contemporary reality. (This is true even of a number of poems about the writer's private world.) There are countervailing forces: Inevitably the poetry situates itself in this time and place through that nuancing which dates all language to particular historical situations, and the more so because of Ondaatje's reliance on a kind of objective immediacy of language. But it is still necessary to view much of Ondaatje's work as, in a crucial sense, a denial. Even the domestic or personal references bear this tension since their scope is carefully limited, with a distorting effect which translates them into something out of the ordinary or (more accurately) out of everyday valuations of intersubjectivity. (The title "Kim, at half an inch" suggests this deliberate search for a perspective which is beyond explicit moral judgments or an aesthetic of feeling.) The archetypal or ideal subjectivity of the 'unconscious,' where it is suggested, is no less alien. Even the elegy for his father's death, "Letters & Other Worlds," seems to work, in part, because his father is an unknown: "His body was a town we never knew."

On one level at least, the denial of easy, clear, implicit or explicit references to the reality frames of the everyday is a refusal to permit the art of language to be bound up with the instrumentalized and debased language which, for the most part, makes up the 'communications' around us. Every writer with a stake in the creative import of language must deal with this issue, which is intensified by media, advertising, and institutionalized learning in our corporate society. Ondaatje's solution to the problem – and no writer's solution to it is ever completely satisfactory – is a kind of objectivist aesthetic which has a long history. One of its most important historical expressions is the aesthetic idealism of Schiller, and such an aesthetic remains necessarily idealist in character. This is one reason why the oppositions of *The Man with Seven Toes* to Ondaatje's own condition are not, from the writer's perspective, self-defeating or question-begging in a negative sense.

In Schiller's writings it is possible to see the links of an objective aesthetics to other core philosophical issues in a way which is perhaps as useful for criticism as anything written since. The integrity of the artwork, responded to aesthetically, is related in Schiller to the universality of the ideal, to the autonomy and freedom of humanity realized in the individual, and to the mediation, in aesthetic experience, of sensuous and intellectual polarities. All of these metaphysical supports for the artwork may be found, implicitly, in Ondaatje.

The oppositions noted previously are comprehensible when it is understood that *The Man with Seven Toes* not only moves toward universality (however that might be translated in current critical rhetoric) but begins from the assumption that universality of aesthetic response is possible. (As Ondaatje prescribes in another poem, "And that is all this writing should be then. / The beautiful formed things caught at the wrong moment / so they are shapeless, awkward/ moving to the clear." Even if there is a suggestion of aesthetic pessimism, the idealism is unmistakable.) It is also possible to see, throughout *The Man with Seven Toes,* the tension between the material conditions – limits imposed by environment and passions – and the poet's distancing, the expression of an autonomous experience and of imaginative release from the codes of our culture. Ondaatje's *Billy the Kid* and *Coming Through Slaughter* return to this kind of evocation with more complexity and insight.

2. *The Man with Seven Toes* presents, almost stanza by stanza, a self-conscious mediation between senses and intellect. Consideration of this process introduces complex questions of how language is shaped by the oppositions of the poem and of why the language, seemingly grounded outside intersubjectivity, is finally evocative. In the next chapters, I will attempt to give a plausible basis for this kind of exploration of context.

Here, returning to the relation between anecdote and poem, it can be said that, whatever the poem's source of inspiration, the writing hardly attempts a translation of a real event – say, a translation from objective history to objective art. Though some sections are intended to be narrated by a Mrs. Fraser character, the style of narration does not vary; there is no attempt to capture a period voice consistently, even if a word or phrase does suggest an attitude of the times. (Ondaatje's protagonist does seem to coincide with period sensibility in describing the aborigines as "Fanatically thin, / black ropes of muscle.") There is no attempt in the poem to 'anthropologize' the aborigines; they are presented through a series of behavioral descriptions which magnify the repulsiveness of their animality.

and the men rip flesh tearing, the muscles
nerves green and red still jumping
stringing them out, like you

and put their heads in
and catch quick quick come on
COME ON! the heart still beating
shocked into death, and catch the heart still running
in their hard quiet lips and eat it alive
alive still in their mouths throats still beating Bang
still! BANG in their stomachs (16)

This is closer to the Hollywood caricature of the primitive than to either the aborigines themselves or the likely sensibility of a captive. Ondaatje might have attempted to mitigate the unreality of this in a couple of ways; he might have renounced the poetic voice of the poem for more consistent Victorian sensationalism or he might have indicated the aborigines' humanity by providing some insight into their cultural space. Whether such possibilities were considered and rejected (an Ondaatje interview in *Rune* seems to suggest they were), it is clear that historical and cultural qualifications would have meant a different sort of poem, and that in *The Man with Seven Toes,* it is aesthetic which takes precedence in the shaping of language.

Again, following Schiller's model (and the Kantian influence in Schiller), the artwork must satisfy on a level of non-utilitarian, undogmatic response. Schiller complains,

Utility is the great idol of the time, to which all powers do homage and all subjects are subservient. In this great balance on utility, the spiritual service of art has no weight, and, deprived of all encouragement, it vanishes from the noisy Vanity Fair of our time. The very spirit of philosophical inquiry itself [read: scientific inquiry] robs the imagination of one promise after another, and the frontiers of art are narrowed in proportion as the limits of science are enlarged.[5]

The complaint is still a reasonable one, perhaps more so now than in Schiller's time, since the spirit of scientific inquiry has become a masquerade for corporate interests and language itself has become a universal medium of exchange in the instrumentalization of culture at all levels. And yet such considerations do not fully set to rights the aesthetic choices in *The Man with Seven Toes*. It is necessary to be aware of the everyday deceptions of language in order to achieve an apparently free work of the imagination, and it is questionable that in portraying aborigines, unnamed muscular primitives, as a blind force, Ondaatje's poem has avoided the suggestion of racial and cultural clichés which were quite outside intended meanings. If the artwork ought to offer a liberating sense of the possibilities of the human spirit, and so ought to avoid dogmatically factual or prescriptive expression, the artist must, nevertheless, understand a good deal about such expression in order to avoid its influences.

3. There is, however, a complex sense of the evocation of the language in a reading of the poem. In provoking an imaginative response, in arousing our interest in the nature of the existence of the poem in our response, *The Man with Seven Toes* succeeds. The technique which is the source of this impact is evident in all of Ondaatje's poetry, though it seems particularly powerful in the longer poems. To understand how the poetry works, it is necessary to push beyond the statics of context to the dynamics of a phenomenological criticism.

CHAPTER THREE

The Role of Imagination in Ondaatje's Poetry

ALL OF Michael Ondaatje's critics, it seems, have wanted to account for the imaginative force of his work, if only in passing. It is a good deal easier to assign the imagery to conventional sources in literary history than to come to terms with the way in which it is experienced. Still, because the imagery is what makes so much of the poetry work, because the imagery is *how* the poetry works when it is effective, reviewers and critics must at least suggest the extraordinary moments that are there in the reading even while trying out the standard litcrit labels. Ondaatje's poetry offers an insight into the way we experience which is more significant (in reception) than his specific choices of subject matter. This is what makes the reduction of context and the narrowness of aesthetic perspective tolerable, especially in *The Collected Works of Billy the Kid* and a large number of poems in *Rat Jelly* but also, to some extent, in *The Man with Seven Toes* and the earlier poems.

Narrative line or descriptive passage does not flow smoothly from point A to point B in Ondaatje's work. The language moves, instead, from pulse to pulse, each pulse being a vividly imaged condensation of relationships, striking in its completeness and in its evocation. As Frank Davey has pointed out, the remarks attributed to the early photographer L.A. Hoffman in *Billy the Kid* suggest the technical movement of Ondaatje's own use of imagery:

I am making daily experiments now and find I am able to take passing horses at a lively trot square across the line of fire – bits of snow in the air – spokes well defined – some blur on top of wheel but sharp in the main – men walking are no trick – I will send you proofs sometime.

The paradox is that, as the imagery moves to greater definition, moves "to the clear," its suggestion of the movement it defines becomes more intense, more precise.

One approach to the phenomenological metamessage of

Ondaatje's imagery is certainly to compare the structure of this word imagery with the structure of various kinds of photographic image. However, what I would like to place some emphasis on is not only the 'frames' of the imagery but what, in reception, lies between the 'frames.' A good starting point for this discussion, especially valuable because it immediately suggests the historical dimensions of the topic, is a consideration of the kinship between Ondaatje's achievement and the classical, medieval and renaissance memory systems. The technical function of such systems (which was never really separable from their rhetorical, scholastic, artistic or religious purposes) was to enable the practitioner to absorb, recall and manipulate a great deal of information, often of very diverse kinds. The development of mnemonic technique required the use of imagery in a way which had been set down by classical writers on rhetoric. Frances Yates provides an excellent discussion of this in *The Art of Memory*; she summarizes:

The artificial memory is established from places and images ..., the stock definition to be forever repeated down the ages. A *locus* is a place easily grasped by the memory, such as a house, an intercolumnar space, a corner, an arch, or the like. Images are forms, marks or simulacra ... of what we wish to remember. For instance if we wish to recall the genus of a horse, of a lion, of an eagle, we must place their images on definite *loci*.[1]

Clearly, both the absorption of *loci* and the working up of specific images for specific meanings involve an exercise in what nowadays would be called eidetic imagery – that is, a structured, vivid imagery which can, under unusual conditions, be mistaken for perception.[2]

There is a special relationship between the *loci* and the assigned images (*imagines*) of the mnemonic system. The *loci* are permanent features of the system and should be many in number to facilitate the absorption and recall of much information.

It is better to form one's memory *loci* in a deserted and solitary place for crowds of passing people tend to weaken the impressions....

Memory *loci* should not be too much like one another, for instance too many intercolumnar spaces are not good, for their resemblance to one another will be confusing. They should be of moderate size, not too large for this renders the images placed on them vague, and not too small for then an arrangement of images will be overcrowded. They must not be too brightly lighted ...; nor must they be too dark.... The intervals between the *loci* should be of moderate extent, perhaps about thirty feet....[3]

The last prescriptions refer to the practise of developing a memory system from the *loci* offered by a single building or by adjacent buildings. Much of Yates' discussion in *The Art of Memory* and the subsequent *Theatre of the World* deals with the use of theatres in the development of memory systems. The image representing a specific content to be committed to memory is not to be confused with a monadic mental image; it is something which is structured, built-up in imagination, composed, typically, of "human figures dramatically engaged in some activity" which is "beautiful or hideous, comic or obscene." The gestures and situations presented in such images are accompanied by the number of elements (specific symbols) necessary to retain the structure of what is being committed to memory. What is committed to memory is the result of the creative work of imagination and, above all, must be as unique and unforgettable as possible in the experience of the practitioner.

Ondaatje's poetry does not (so far as I know) derive from or represent a memory system, but the structure of its imagery does bear a striking resemblance to the products of this creative mnemonics. Where the poems give a sense of place, the place is often a frame or architectonic background for image or images which are active, vivid, sensual, sometimes repulsive, painful or violent. Like the *loci* of the memory technique described above, the places of the poems are, for the most part, familiar and uncluttered structures which serve to locate the central images. This treatment of place is already evident in the first book, *The Dainty Monsters*. "A House Divided" situates its imagery through *house* in the title. In "A Toronto Home for Birds and Manticores" the *locus* is simply "this city with sun spreading down the street" with the modest qualifier "when snows have melted." In "Paris" the *locus* of the first section does not become complex by being offered piecemeal and with a certain suspense. Ondaatje finally encompasses it in a phrase anyway: "At night it is cold on the mountain".

The *loci* of *The Man with Seven Toes* are, if anything, generally sparer in structure than those of *The Dainty Monsters*. In some segments of the poem, where place is assumed from previous segments, the imagery seems to be all 'foreground,' as in

Our best meal was two pale green eggs
we sucked the half flesh out
salt liquid spilling
drying white on our shoulders. (30)

The remoteness of setting (as well as the orientation to dramatic performance) imposes a reduction of place-structure throughout, and when place is established, this is invariably done in a very few words. Several examples from different segments may give an indication:

1. into the plain (26)
2. ... the river, frail
   as nerves in the desert
   the banks pocked with hoof trails. (28)
3. Evening. Sky was a wrecked black boot
   a white world spilling through.
   Noise like electricity in the leaves. (32)
4. next to a mountain (36)
5. entered the clearing (11)

Surprisingly, the schematic character of the *loci* seems to enhance the vivid imagery in the 'foreground' of the narrative. Perhaps the *loci,* in their generality, evoke the non-rigorous memory of places by which we still recognize, and live in relation to, a great deal of our experience.

The least successful writing in *The Man with Seven Toes* ignores the unity of the *locus* and, moving outside the *locus*-imagery structure, attempts to bring description-without-a-subject to the fore:

Sun disappears after noon
after the purple glare
clashes down the side of trees.
Then swamp is blue
green, the mist
sitting like toads.
Leaves spill snakes
their mouths arched
with bracelets of teeth.
Once a bird, silver
with arm wide wings
flew a trail between trees
and never stopped,
caught all the sun
and spun like mercury away from us. (23)

The problem here is that the poetry offers neither a satisfactory scheme of objective description nor a coherence of gesture and mood originating with the protagonist.

In *Rat Jelly,* perhaps half of the poems do not use a simple *locus*-imagery structure. Among these are poems taking the form of letters ("Letter to Ann Landers," "To Monsieur le Maire"), poems about art ("'The gate in his head,'" "King Kong meets Wallace Stevens"), portraits ("Notes for the Legend of Salad Woman," "War Machine"), surreal recollections ("Dates," "Letters & Other Worlds"), and characterizations of animals ("Loop," "Flirt and Wallace"). In a few poems, such as "Leo" and "Rat Jelly," the *locus*-imagery structure is there but it is ambiguous. The abrupt shift in "Leo" from the *locus* bed to the implicit *locus* of a room with sinks and mirrors where prisoners shave causes some difficulty in reception, in putting the two parts of the poem together. This suggests the strength and weakness of the *locus,* its strength being that it provides a concise and unobtrusive 'frame' for an imagery which is intended to have immediacy and its weakness being that its very precision may tend to overdefine a particular moment or movement of thought. Unfortunately, the ambiguity of *locus* is underscored in this poem by Ondaatje's leaving the shift in *locus* implicit.

Nineteen[A] of the forty poems in *Rat Jelly* have a clearly identifiable *locus,* which may be given explicitly or implicitly. The seeming domesticity of much of the book is reflected in the *loci*; house, cabin, room, bedroom, kitchen and mattress are *loci* in eleven of the nineteen poems. Quite in contrast to the *locus*-imagery of these poems are the poems "Looking into THE PROJECTOR" and "Burning Hills," which turn the function of *locus* back on itself in interesting ways.

The projector itself is the familiar *locus* of "Looking into THE PROJECTOR," and the imagery of disorientation and movement suggests looking into a projector and taking up certain images in unexpected ways. The opening lines launch us into this uncanniness:

The horse is falling off the skyscraper
staggering through the air
He will never reach
pavements of men and cars,
he is caught between
the 70th and 72nd floor of someone's brain. (*RJ* 59)

A These are: "Gold and Black," "Kim, at half an inch," "Somebody sent me a tape," "Postcard from Picadilly Street," "White Room," "Griffin of the night," "Breaking Green," "Philoctetes on the island," "Stuart's bird," "The Ceremony: A Dragon, a Hero, and a Lady, by Uccello," "Near Elginburg," "Burning Hills," "Looking into THE PROJECTOR," "Fabulous Shadow," "Spider Blues," "Birth of Sound."

Staggering returns us to the movement of film through a projector as does the suggestion that what is seen is both absurd and concocted (film). Repeatedly, we are brought back to the *locus* – for example, with the indication of the jerking movement of the film in "bobbing dobbin" and with the explicit transition "a few frames later" as well as the closing ironic reference to the horse's rider, another creature of the absurd events inside the machine:

The air is moving the wrong way in him
he will be consumed before ever reaching the ground.

Whatever the events on film, the rider will also be consumed as spectacle.

The poem "Burning Hills" – about the mindspace of a writer in summer retreat – is significant for Ondaatje's use of a *locus*-imagery structure since the imagery of the poem not only has its *locus* in a cabin ("in the burnt hill region / north of Kingston") but within the cabin there are *loci,* present and absent, of the experience which is the subject matter of the poem. Of course these are the *loci* of memory:

Eventually the room was a time machine for him.
He closed the rotting door, sat down
thought pieces of history. (59)

The *loci* of memory are compared to "old photographs he didn't look at anymore" and then a single photograph is recalled with particular completeness:

There is one picture that fuses the 5 summers.
Eight of them are leaning against a wall
arms around each other
looking into the camera and the sun
trying to smile at the unseen adult photographer
trying against the glare to look 21 and confident. (58)

The image has a clear and evident structure, and its nostalgia is both feeling and mechanical, which captures the uncanny evenhandedness of an old photograph. In its vividness, the clear relation of persons and things to each other, the recollection of the photograph works like a specific creation in a classical memory system: "one picture that fuses the 5 summers."

The setting of *Billy the Kid,* as in the earlier longer narrative poems, is remote – the American Southwest of the 1880s, and again

Ondaatje does not really attempt to give a sense of that place in that time. The premising of historical place is more evocative than in the earlier works because, thanks to pop art, we have come to 'understand' that particular environment almost by reflex. (This has its irony, for one of Ondaatje's purposes in *Billy the Kid* was to overturn, or turn inside out, certain pop art clichés.) Put a horse and rider before us in the narrative, and we may see them on the writer's terms; but we may also, spontaneously, accept the suggestions of imagination, regardless of what the page says. This is part of that realm of illusion which Ondaatje pointedly draws attention to in the Western fairytale at the end of the piece.

That elements of setting in *Billy the Kid* are evocative, then, does not mean that they are any less schematic. At the same time, by using a general (though artificial) setting with many more compartments or niches for experience, Ondaatje opts for a structure which facilitates the development of images and the imaginative experience of their relations more readily than this was accomplished in the earlier works.

Again, it is interesting to consider together *loci* given in different segments of the book:

1. Fort Sumner, 1880 (*BK* 7)
2. moving across the world on horses (11)
3. Blurred a waist high river
   foam against the horse (14)
4. The barn I stayed in for a week then was at the edge of a farm and had been deserted it seemed for several years, though built of stone and good wood. (17)
5. I take in all the angles of the room (21)
6. Forty miles ahead of us, in almost a straight line, is the house. (32)

As in *The Man with Seven Toes,* there are narrative segments which do not give their *loci* explicitly but rely on the description in previous, related segments or present situations which evoke place. (An example of the latter is the segment beginning "To be near flowers in the rain.") There are more elaborate suggestions of place than the examples above may indicate. The writing about the barn in which Billy stays for a week, about the Mescalaro territory in August, and about the Chisums' verandah involves a subtle and rich interrelating of persons and places although, significantly, each segment is contained within its *locus* and, discursively, is closer to the sort of narrative we associate with the novel.

The foregoing should serve to give an idea of the schematic, often architectonic place-references which 'frame' or ground the central images of the poetry. What is the role of these images in the *locus*-imagery structure? Serious attention has been devoted to the existential and supposed myth-making significance of the subject matter of the imagery and due notice taken repeatedly of the imagery's liveliness, its sensuality and violence. But not much has been said about its values as technique. The example of classical mnemonics provides a means of approaching this subject. Recall the characteristics required of the image to be placed on a *locus* of a memory system. According to Cicero, the image must be "active, sharply defined, unusual" and must have "the power of speedily encountering and penetrating the psyche."[4] The writer of *Ad Herennium* explained:

Now nature herself teaches us what we should do. When we see in everyday life things that are petty, ordinary, and banal, we generally fail to remember them, because the mind is not being stirred by anything novel or marvellous. But if we see or hear something exceptionally base, dishonourable, unusual, great, unbelievable, or ridiculous, that we are likely to remember for a long time.[5]

That three of the six adjectives in the series ("exceptionally base, dishonourable ... ridiculous") are pejorative is no accident. The creative intention in the development of mnemonic imagery must be the ordering of a content through a unique structure, and the everyday moral polarity of the elements of that structure is irrelevant. "There are no dirty words – ever." Through the classical prescription for a good memory, it is possible to see how a polite language and a transparent literature create the basis for their own extinction.

The structure and attributes of the images in the poems following the *locus*-imagery pattern is necessarily a more complex subject than the identification of *loci* in these poems. For purposes of illustration, therefore, I've limited the examples to two poems from *Rat Jelly* and two segments from *Billy the Kid*.

A short poem which illustrates the *locus*-imagery relation in Ondaatje's work particularly well is "Philoctetes on the island," the *locus* being the island of the title. The poem is a series of images placed on the *locus*, interrelated by it but monadic in their precision.

The first image moves from distance to foreground in a careful focusing for emphasis:

Sun moves broken in the trees
drops like a paw
turns sea to red leopard

I trap sharks and drown them
stuffing gills with sand
cut them with coral till
the blurred grey runs
red designs

With an awareness that this is a unitary image, we can see the recapitulation in "designs" of the pattern of sun described in the first lines.
 The next lines perhaps suggest at first reading a departure from the *locus*-imagery relation, but the reference to ego underscores the significance of the first image and the attitude of reflection is the vehicle of transition to each subsequent image. Thus the second image decisively returns to the *locus*:

to leave all pity on the staggering body
in order not to shoot an arrow up
and let it hurl
down through my petalling skull (*RJ* 34)

Consider these first images in terms of the technique of mnemonics. The elements of each image are sharply defined in that the labelling of them is simple and obvious – *sun, trees, gills, skull, eye*; and the elements are active and penetrating both because the verbs and verbals relating them are active and because the labels themselves have, in some cases, an active suggestiveness: *paw, sharks, skull*. The elements in movement become an imagery which is novel, violent and repelling (about which Ondaatje manages to be simultaneously malicious and self-deprecating when he says, elsewhere in the book, "I want you to know it's rat / steamy dirty hair and still alive"). Even the first lines of "Philoctetes," which might have suggested a natural occurrence at one remove from the "I" of the poem, present a metaphor of the sun as leopard, raking the sea with its paw. A succession of verbs – *trap, drown, cut, kill, shoot, hurl, shoot, catch* – link all elements of the images in a "nightmare's chain." The insistence on violence becomes itself repelling and enhances the graphic impact of the images, but there are immediately repelling elements as well: the imaginary arrow "through my petalling skull / or neck vein"; the alternative to reflection, "Shoot either eye of bird instead / and run and catch it in your hand."

There is surely nothing very unexpected about violent imagery in a poem metaphorically drawing upon the story of an archer of the Trojan War (although Sophocles' play about Philoctetes on Lemnos is concerned with his "suffering, his humiliation, and his helpless ineffectuality"[6] rather than with violent character). However, if the poem is interpreted only on the level of characterization, there is a kind of sensationalism in the writing which is difficult to see as necessary. The violence of the language, then, has a repetitious, mechanical quality which, beyond a certain point, ceases to illuminate character. As well, the opening lines suggest, on this level of reading, the improbability that either the character's obsession extends to hurling metaphors at sunsets or the writer felt that we would not sufficiently gather from the rest of the poem that it concerns itself with violent emotions. I think that a more appropriate reading must take into account the *locus*-imagery structure of the work and that, when Ondaatje's technical approach is clear, some of the absurdities of interpretation can be avoided.

"Kim, at half an inch" is a shorter poem from *Rat Jelly,* which contrasts in mood with "Philoctetes on the island" but also possesses the characteristics of a good mnemonic image:

Brain is numbed
is body touch
and smell, warped light

hooked so close
her left eye
is only a golden blur
her ear a vast
musical instrument of flesh

The *locus* of the poem is implicit and obvious – a bedroom at night, and the first lines provide an orientation (of sensation) for the image within the *locus,* giving a relation to the elements of the image in the brain of a half-awake poet-observer. Each of the elements is active.

The proximity of "hooked" and "eye" is charged even if the relation between the words is oblique in a logical reading; the ear metamorphoses from an organ of "passive" reception to become "a vast / musical instrument of flesh." Its primary association is struck away, and it becomes something else, a startling shape "at half an inch." The final lines use the overforcefulness of "spills" and "slides" as a foil which underscores the peace of the sleeper:

The moon spills off my shoulder
slides into her face (16)

There is no question that each of the elements of the image – eye, ear, moonlight on observer and sleeper – has been made to appear under an unusual aspect.

The segment beginning "With the Bowdres" in *Billy the Kid* also uses a room for *locus,* and two images are placed on the *locus,* one enclosing the other:

She is boiling us black coffee
leaning her side against the warm stove
taps her nails against the mug
Charlie talking on about things
and with a bit the edge of my eye
I sense the thin white body of my friend's wife

Strange that how I feel people
not close to me
as if their dress were against my shoulder
and as they bend down
the strange smell of their breath
moving across my face
or my eyes
magnifying the bones across a room
shifting in a wrist (*BK* 39)

The first stanza develops the first image, each of the initial four lines conveying an element of it and the concluding two lines bringing the elements into a conscious unity. This structure of inchoate feeling, however, becomes self-consciousness mixed with fantasy in the second stanza, producing a new image which is bracketed by the analytical reflection preceding it and following it in the last two lines of the poem. Although the language of the first lines is not unusual, it is precise and it is the language of activity; the element of novelty here enters through suspense when we realize that, much as in movie westerns in which placid shots must erupt into action, these first lines have a focus, an ambiguous intention relating the "I" to the people observed. When the poem returns to this scene at the end, a new element of perception is added which fuses the others in an unexpected conclusion: "magnifying the bones across a room / shifting in a wrist".

The prose narrative of the night which Billy and Angela spend at the Chisums' with Garrett moves through several changes of mood and situation but opens with the group on the Chisums' front porch in a description which has an evident *locus*-imagery structure. The initial image treats each character as a figure in a group portrait. There is some difficulty representing so many complex elements within the scope of an image. Ondaatje's solution, only partially successful, is to develop with precision a number of vivid details, such as those in the lines:

... our bodies out here blocking out sections of the dark night. And the burn from the kerosene lamp throwing ochre across our clothes and faces. John in the silent rocking chair bending forward and back, one leg tucked under him, with each tilt his shirt smothering the light and spiralling shadows along the floor. (67)

The problem is that the figures on the verandah must have not only different thoughts but different postures and attitudes and that there is no single, sweeping intention which pulls them all into necessary relation within an image. Paradoxically, Billy reflects that "the Chisum verandah is crowded"; this refers, of course, to the matter of the subsequent reminiscence but the *locus* is, in fact, an overcrowded space because the space has not been sufficiently differentiated. Whatever the alleged size of the Chisums' verandah, it is only one place in the *locus*-imagery relation.

*

Thus far I have attempted to indicate a recurring structure in Ondaatje's poetry without going very much further into why I think that structure works. It would, no doubt, be possible to find numerous, rather mechanical variations on the analysis given above;

there is a kind of academic structuralism which revels in this sort of exercise while ignoring those concerns which make literature something more than a hobby or a profession.

Again, mnemonics provides a suggestion of direction. Because of the practical relation of memory systems and the arts, it was perhaps inevitable that there should be a fusion of the notion of mnemonic images with a theory of imagination. This fusion took place in the thought of Giordano Bruno.

In Bruno's memory art, there is (in Frances Yates' words) a "truly extraordinary Renaissance and Hermetic transformation" of classical mnemonics, a transformation in which the memory system becomes "the vehicle for the formation of the psyche of a Hermetic mystic and magus."[7] Bruno's memory systems take their order from the topographical orders of Lullism and astrology, and his prescriptions for the formation of images within these systems combines the recipe of classical mnemonics with the magical requirement that the images must be shadows, the earthly signs, of divine ideas:

Bruno believes that if he can make a system which gets inside the astrological system, which reflects the permutations and combinations of the changing relations of the planets to the zodiac and their influences on the horoscopal houses, he will be tapping the mechanisms of nature herself to organize the psyche.[8]

But if the ultimate aim of Bruno's memory systems is a certain relation to the cosmos, it is, nevertheless, necessary to propose a dynamic of thought, a glue which binds the images together and works those transformations of psyche which reflect the divine mind.

Since the divine mind is universally present in the world of nature ... the process of coming to know the divine mind must be through the reflection of the images of the world of sense within the *mens*. Therefore the function of the imagination of ordering the images in memory is an absolutely vital one in the cognitive process.[9]

As I've indicated earlier, the efficacy of classical mnemonics raises questions about how it works. The classical answer, from Aristotle, was "to think is to speculate with images." In twentieth-century debate over mind, even that much has been omitted in many views when it has seemed more important to establish the possibility of systematic and rigorous thought. But Bruno goes beyond Aristotle in the other direction; he does not see images as mere elements in the logical matrix of thought. "There is for Bruno no separate faculty consisting of the abstracting intellect; the mind works only with images, though these images are of different degrees of potency."[10]

To accept the full implications of that, for criticism, for all our thinking about thinking, requires a revaluation of ideological habits which permeate our cultural life. And it is not possible simply to look up the answers in the work of Giordano Bruno. Though Brunians opposed Ramists in the sixteenth century, underlying the development of Bruno's work (which looks toward a religion and politics of magic rather than an operational logic) is a mathesis of signs which not only resembles Ramist method in its search for rigor but also anticipates the reduction of cosmos to order in the Cartesian system. Thus Bruno's thought carries the very biases and anticipations which, in subsequent periods, result in the submergence of the question of imagination.

From Frances Yates' account of Bruno, it can be understood, in a general way, how the combination of *loci* and *imagines* may be something other than a means of expressing or recalling vivid impressions. The necessary sequel to an analysis of Ondaatje's poetry in terms of *locus*-imagery structure must be to understand, in reception, how a synthesis of the individual pulses of imagery takes place. *Imaginative* and *imagination* are frequently recurring terms in the reviews and critical estimates of Ondaatje's work, but the labels offer too much and too little. The words are debased by a long history which has excluded them from the practical and the instrumental and, on the other hand, have been assimilated to a rhetoric of creativity, subjectivity and aesthetic which has subordinated its truth to scientific ideology and 'objective necessity.' But the reviewers and critics are right: There is something in Ondaatje's work which strongly suggests that imagination has its domain, that its sleight-of-hand works in us even if we've been taught to think by the rules. However, it is important to uncover a sense of the term *imagination* which will make evident just why Ondaatje's work has this kind of impact. The starting point is given in Bruno's mnemonics − in Frances Yates' words, "the mind works only in images."

*

In accepting Bruno's view of imagination as a vital clue to the nature of thinking and then, specifically, to the effectiveness of Ondaatje's poetry, I do not mean to indicate that a primarily metaphysical description is forthcoming, something which would reveal (in the manner of Heidegger perhaps) more fundamental and absolute terms in which to couch the problems of existence. In this discussion, *imagination* labels a complex process; even if it is freighted with too limiting and contradictory meanings, it is still the everyday term which most nearly represents the process to be described. The complex process, imagination, is outlined in a phenomenological style of discourse, which means language attempting to follow the contours of experience, including the historical ones, in the recognition of the inevitable uncertainties, ambiguities and political nature of discourse.

To begin to get at this sense of imagination as thought, I want to recapitulate, briefly, the history of imagination from Bruno to Schiller; I believe that there are some surprising clues in this history to our own repression of imagination's potentials and to our inability to use imagination effectively as a critical concept.

Bruno lived and wrote at a critical moment in the history of imagination. The most familiar chapter of the crisis is probably the rising opposition to poetry and the theatre, which largely owed their existence to an aristocratic ideal which was out of favor with the newly arrived merchants, manufacturers and agrarian capitalists. In English literature, there is even a date which sets a period to the decisive phase of the opposition: 1642, the closing of English theatres by law.

The Jacobean businessman, who measures utility in terms of avoirdupois, is sufficiently coarse; Max Weber might have invented him. The preacher, whose criteria are ethical and moral, is not so obvious in formulating his indictment. The scientist and social critic – Galileo, Jean Bodin, to whom poetry is ephemeral and therefore indifferent – are more elusive than the preacher. But the gravamen of these various objections is the same. Poetry, which takes a mess of shadows for its meat, is rejected as it is useless.[11]

The language of most value to the new society was instrumental, whether in the relation between believer and God or in the transactions of money-making and the new science.

Still, imagination remained an important part of philosophical explanation throughout the seventeenth century; as R.G. Collingwood points out,

To most of the seventeenth-century philosophers it seemed clear that all sensation is simply imagination. The common-sense distinction was simply wiped out, and the existence of anything which could be called real sensation was denied. It was admitted that our sensa are caused by the action upon our bodies of other bodies (of whose existence we were assured not, of course, by sensation but by thought), but the fact that imagination has an external cause does not make it any the less imagination.[12]

Such a philosophical orientation is difficult to comprehend in twentieth-century terms if only because the notion of systematic and certain knowledge of an external world is inculcated early. (Without a critique of this style of learning and knowing and its implications for creating, it would be well-nigh impossible either to see the vitality in what Bruno, Hobbes and Spinoza have to say about imagination or to grasp the imaginative process itself. This critique is taken up in Chapter 4.)

After the seventeenth century, the most influential reconsideration of imagination was probably the synthesizing imagination of Kant's *Critique of Pure Reason*, especially in its first edition.[13] Schiller and other Romantics picked up on Kant's aesthetic and, stimulated by it but not limited by it, reworked the whole question in different ways. Schiller's approach is the most interesting, perhaps, because it maintains the tensions which permit us to see what the problem of imagination was and why it could not be resolved at that time.

For Schiller, imagination and understanding have essentially opposed functions: "It is the interest of the imagination to change objects according to its caprice; the interest of the understanding is to unite its representations with strict logical necessity." Nevertheless, Schiller also found dangers in the exclusion of one by the other:

That which flatters our senses in immediate sensation opens our weak and volatile spirit to every impression, but makes us in some degree less apt for exertion. That which stretches our thinking power and invites to abstract conceptions strengthens our mind for every kind of resistance, but it hardens it also in the same proportion, and deprives us of susceptibility in the same ratio that it helps us to greater mental activity.[14]

Schiller is probably more concerned with the rigidity of understanding and everyday morality than with the caprices of imagination; early in the *Letters on the Aesthetical Education of Man,* he argues,

... in our day it is necessity, neediness, that prevails, and bends a degraded humanity under its iron yoke. *Utility* is the great idol of the time, to which all powers do homage and all subjects are subservient. In this great balance on utility, the spiritual service of art has no weight, and deprived of all encouragement, it vanishes from the noisy Vanity Fair of our time.[15]

Clearly, however, the polarity between the imagination and understanding is necessary because, by definition, imagination alone is not responsible in a world which strives after a systematic moral outlook – a moral law parallel to, and rationalizable in terms of, natural law, which in turn reflects the operationalism and instrumental necessities of economic life.

Schiller fuses imagination and understanding in a dialectic of aesthetic sensibility; it is this fusion which gives rise to his conception of *play* as its dynamic expression and to the famous dictum: "... man only plays when in the full meaning of the word he is a man, and *he is only completely a man when he plays*."[16] Though Schiller must give the upper hand to morality, which represses "the sensuous instinct" and which is shaped by the understanding and commanded by reason, he, nevertheless, moves very far toward giving imagination an equal role in the development of a human character which can realize freedom – a political, even a utopian passion in Schiller's work:

If in the dynamic state of rights men mutually move and come into collision as forces, in the moral (ethical) state of duties, man opposes to man the majesty of the laws, and chains down his will. In this realm of the beautiful or the aesthetic state, man ought to appear to man only as a form, and an object of free play. To give freedom through freedom is the fundamental law of this realm.[17]

The dialectical expression of this political aim both elevates the imagination and suggests an inescapable dilemma for Schiller:

A very refined aesthetical education accustoms the imagination to *direct itself according to laws, even in its free exercise,* and leads the sensuous not to have enjoyments without the concurrence of reason; but it soon follows that reason, in its turn, is required to be directed, even in the most *serious operations of its legislative power, according to the interests of imagination,* and to give no more orders to the will without the consent of the sensuous instincts.[18]

The dilemma appears again and again in Schiller's writings on aesthetics: Having given the liberating values of imagination and the

arts a new, political importance in the struggle for individual freedom, how is it possible to maintain moral law in its position of
supremacy? We see in the passage above that Schiller even demurs
from the absolute moral efficacy of Kantian reason.

Thus, in spite of its importance as an instrument of freedom, in
spite of its role in the humanizing dialectic of play, imagination cannot be the fundamental process of thinking. It must be subordinated,
finally to the systematicity of morality, and, tellingly, Schiller
excludes it from an essential role in scientific argument – "In a
scientific lecture the senses are altogether set aside...."[19] – while
conceding that this does violence to sensibility:

The understanding observes a strict necessity and conformity with laws in its
combinations, and it is only the consistent connection of ideas that satisfies
it. ... The poetic impulse of imagination must be curbed by distinctness of
expression, and its capricious tendency must be limited by a strictly legitimate course of procedure. I grant that it will not bend to this yoke without
resistance; but in this matter reliance is properly placed on a certain self-
denial, and on an earnest determination of the hearer or reader not to be
deterred by the difficulties accompanying the form, for the sake of the
subject-matter.[20]

The fact that the impulses of imagination are at odds with the order
imposed by understanding does not push Schiller to the question of
whether this repression is necessary or to the still more remote question of whether imagination may not be inherently anarchic (within
the a priori categories of space and time). Schiller does not go on to
these questions because to do so would require the overturning (in
thought!) of pervasive and coinciding natural, moral, and economic
orders which determine the operational code of society and, therefore, are the tacit or explicit means by which the truth-value of any
discourse in Schiller's time is asserted. Even as he realizes the liberating values of art, therefore, Schiller must hold to a moral order and to
a scientific ideology which are essentially oppressive, fully aware of
the violence done to imagination but, in the spirit of the times, capable of rationalizing that as serving higher ends.

*

Throughout Ondaatje's work, it seems to me, the violence of the
imagery represents not only a certain technique but also the release
of imagination from this oppression. In Billy the Kid, this tension

itself becomes subject matter for the poetry and, with other oppositions, a reference scheme of the narrative. Early in the book there is a
prose account of Billy's stay (as a boy) in a barn during sickness. His
vitality is low (he lies on a makeshift bed for a week) and his awareness opens out to the continuum of birds, insects, patterns of light,
colours, shapes of things in the barn. He enters into an imaginative
relation with these things:

The fly who sat on my arm, after his inquiry, just went away, ate his disease
and kept it in him. When I walked I avoided the cobwebs who had places to
grow to, who had stories to finish. The flies caught in those acrobat nets were
the only murder I saw. (17)

This living in an imagination which is no longer aping the controls of
an atomized and essentially hostile society is brought to an end with
Billy's recovery and the bizarre invasion of rats from a neighboring
granary. The inebriated rats behave savagely because they have
abandoned "sanity." Billy recovers the logic of his reactions and kills
every living thing in the barn "but for the boy in the blue shirt sitting
there coughing at the dust, rubbing the sweat of his upper lip with his
left forearm." The language itself returns to distanced, factual
description.

Throughout *Billy the Kid* imagination reaches out for the violent
will which would overturn the degradation of sensibility which Billy
realizes within it; a strongly focused example is the segment:

White walls neon on the eye
1880 November 23   my birthday

catching flies with my left hand
bringing the fist to my ear
hearing the scream grey buzz
as their legs cramp their
heads with no air
so eyes split and release

open fingers
the air and sun hit them like pollen
sun flood drying them red
catching flies
angry weather in my head, too (58)

The anthropomorphism of the middle lines reveals the projection of Billy himself upon the flies; but he is both the tormentor and the tormented, the imagination erupts in a violent gesture which both creates an angry moment of its own liberation and confirms its own double-bind, its repressed and degraded life as the imagination which chains imagination.

The struggle within imagination is not merely something which takes place in Billy's head; it involves the totality of bodily response as is evident, for example, in brilliantly condensed expression of a range of sensuous response in the segment

Blurred a waist high river
foam against the horse
riding naked clothes and boots
and pistol in the air

Crossed a crooked river
loving in my head
ambled dry on stubble
shot a crooked bird

Held it in my fingers
the eyes were small and far
it yelled out like a trumpet
destroyed it of its fear (14)

Here the violence of imagination springs casually from its momentary sensuous freedom, only to recoil on itself as the language approaches identification of Billy and creature. The identification is both acknowledged and exorcised in Billy's having "destroyed it of its fear."

Bodily response is compromised – repressed, forced into destructive channels – by the double-bind of imagination even though love may, on occasion, take the body beyond this as when Billy discovers that love-making has changed the behavior of his gun hand:

later my hands cracked in love juice
fingers paralysed by it arthritic
these beautiful fingers I couldnt move
faster than a crippled witch now (16)

The more usual state of affairs is a repression of feeling and a mechanical sense of action in others and in the self:

one must eliminate much
that is one turns when the bullet leaves you
walk off see none of the thrashing
the very eyes welling up like bad drains
believing then the moral of newspapers or gun
where bodies are mindless as paper flowers you dont feed
or give to drink
that is why I can watch the stomach of clocks
shift their wheels and pins into each other
and emerge living, for hours (11)

The repressed imagination, when it is calling the shots, as in this passage, echoes, even is a double of, the characterization of Pat Garrett. And yet, in Billy, there is also an imaginative struggle for freedom which fails repeatedly to Billy's isolation and his distrust of the others: "In the end the only thing that never changed, never became deformed, were animals." The caged animals at the Chisums' are living symbols of this struggle and its frustration ("We knew they continued like that all night while we slept."), but the liberating force of imagination is not a matter of a crude opposition in the poetry between animal awareness and human consciousness. (It is significant that Billy finds himself in the skin of an animal – "locked inside my skin sensitive as an hour old animal" – when being moved around as Garrett's prisoner.) The vitality of a liberating imagination is more complex and is suggested by the exuberance of the passage

I am here with the range for everything
corpuscle muscle hair
hands that need the rub of metal
those senses that
that want to crash things with an axe
that listen to deep buried veins in our palms
those who move in dreams over your women night
near you, every paw, the invisible hooves
the mind's invisible blackout   the intricate never
the body's waiting rut (72)

Ondaatje does not overlook that this outpouring, with its positive imaginative force, must reflect Billy's trap ("hands that need the rub of metal"), his automatic violence in his hostile world, and the tenuous hope for salvation in love and lust.

In the last lines of *Billy the Kid*, Ondaatje suggests that he himself is rising not only from "a bad night" but from the dream-like struggle to create, a struggle to liberate the powers of imagination in search of the truth of experience. He has asked us directly to "Imagine if you dug him [Billy] up and brought him out." Billy's legend remains "a jungle sleep" (97) just because it can awaken the terrors and the possibilities of a liberating force in imagination.

CHAPTER FOUR

The Poetry and the Imaginative Process

THE previous chapter indicated a particular view of imagination and offered several applications of the concept to a reading of Michael Ondaatje's poetry. Several important points remain to be covered: a detailed characterization of the imaginative process, a description of how the poetry works through imagination, and an account of the impact and importance which the poetry has in this regard. The view of imagination I am developing here is not an easy one to present in a few pages; the difficulty is that there are some preconceptions to deal with, about consciousness and about what it is to think and to imagine.

The character of Pat Garrett in *Billy the Kid* reveals the repression of an atomized, hostile society, of an abstract but ruthlessly systematic moral law, and of an instrumentalized, mechanical existence. It is, therefore, a good starting point for understanding what must be confronted to understand the imaginative process generally as well as to understand the role of imagination in *Billy the Kid*. The character really has only one dimension, and yet it is recognizable and even evocative as a typification of experience. Pat Garrett is (as I said last chapter) a double of Billy's own repressed imagination and an alien or absurd personality which most of us could find within ourselves (although not always recognizing its otherness or its absurdity). This has been an essential part of our education, the introjection of a rationality which is alien to our own needs and experiences. Significantly, Garrett laughs only when, in a dark room, he is about to shoot Billy, who has mistaken his identity. Reason and order have the last laugh on darkness and uncertainty. In introducing the character earlier, Ondaatje is explicit about Garrett's hostility to Billy's imagination — "usually pointless and never in control." Garrett recognizes Billy's wit but doesn't understand it since it comes from sources which are repressed in himself;

I had expected him to be the taciturn pale wretch – the image of the shallow punk that was usually attached to him by others. The rather cruel smile, when seen close, turned out to be intricate and witty. You could never tell how he meant a phrase, whether he was serious or joking. From his eyes you could tell nothing at all. In general, he had a quick, quiet humour. His only affectation was his outfit of black clothes speckled with silver buttons and silver belt lock. Also his long black hair was pulled back and tied in a knot of leather. (43)

Garrett's description directs our attention to Billy, but we must also be aware that he is describing himself. He cannot get inside the skin of his victim; to do so would surely compromise his own carefully bounded imagination. He recognizes an "intricate" character in Billy but finds it incomprehensible and ends by judging Billy in superficial terms, which clash with his own sense of order. Garrett's only undiluted moment of admiration for Billy comes when Billy has systematically located and killed a poisoned cat under the floorboards of the Chisums' house:

Our faces must have been interesting to see then. John and Sallie [Chisum] were thankful, almost proud of him. I had a look I suppose of incredible admiration for him too. But when I looked at Angie, leaning against the rail of the verandah, her face was terrified. Simply terrified. (45)

Here, again, is an identification of Garrett with Billy's own repression of imagination. In the next section, I will try to indicate, in outline, the sources of this repression and, then, to show how imagination re-emerged as an issue in phenomenology, leading to a phenomenological criticism of imagination.

*

If the character of morality in Europe and European settlements was becoming, in some respects, less rigid in Schiller's time and subsequent periods, the advance of capitalist forms of social organization, hand in hand with the advance of scientific ideology, gave rise to institutions which imposed an even more rigorous and more universal intellectual economy on the creative impulse of imagination. Foremost of these institutions, where the question of the role of imagination is concerned, has been state-sponsored and state-controlled education, which still lags behind the impetus of contemporary feeling in not fully acknowledging a crisis in the explanations of capitalist scientific ideology (even when such explanations are offered in socialist classrooms!).

At the level of a crude but ubiquitous kind of educational administration, the matter of education boils down to a quantification of teaching, of the material to be learned, and of the results achieved by the learner in terms of a wholly instrumentalized ideal of education output: the efficiency of money spent on the production of standardized and appropriate educations for jobs and careers. But the efficacy of institutional education would not be what it is if its objectives did not permeate the subject matter of the classroom as well. As I have pointed out elsewhere,

The question-and-answer in the classroom, which results in the anxiety and failure described by John Holt, is not only the end product of certain social demands built into the educational system; this constant eliciting of answers owes a great deal to the teachers' own belief in a scientifically dogmatized reality. Things are represented to children as part of what Husserl called the 'garb of ideas' – the idealizations of scientific ideology. The things are thereby placed outside the child's own reckoning, his or her capacity to manipulate them in an autodidactic way. Besides what is communicated about things on the most evident level, there is a metalanguage of gesture 'personalizing' scientific ideology. Adults do not relate, generally, to things as if their meaning could change, as if their present associations are contingent, open to the play of ideas; in spite of all the pedagogical talk about teaching children the symbolic character of words, this must be rarely conveyed with any consistency. A word which already belongs to another reality than the child's and the teacher's or parent's is not meaningfully symbolic but absurd.[1]

In this context, recall the photographic symbol – kid in cowboy suit – of Ondaatje's own childhood in *Billy the Kid*: the ironic combination of the play of imagination and the costume of murderous repression. The repression of imagination is pervasive in twentieth-century education, and, to get at it, it's necessary to review the history of scientific ideology in the spirit of recent critiques of it by philosophers of science and phenomenologists.

The claims of scientific ideology to comprehensiveness, coherence and certainty found some opposition even in the heyday of nineteenth-century scientific materialism and amid a flood of popular writings which suggested that there were elegant scientific explanations for just about everything:

994. *Why are the nostrils directed downwards?*
Because, as odours and effluvia ascend, the nose is directed toward them,
and thereby receives the readiest intimation of those bodies floating in the air
which may be pleasurable to the sense, or offensive to the smell, and injuri-
ous to life.[2]

The nineteenth-century opposition, however, came largely from
within or, alternatively, in reaction to scientific claims which had to
be conceded on one level and rejected on another. Much of the
interest in this opposition has, in fact, been generated only in the
twentieth century when it has been possible to see how the criticisms
fit into a more extensive questioning of the ideology. Given the dogmatic education described above, the professional organization of
the sciences, and the vital relation between scientific work and capitalism, it is not surprising that a thorough critique of scientific ideology has only developed in the last twenty-five years. In the field of
history and philosophy of science, some of the key figures in this
period have been N.K. Hanson, Alexandre Koyré (a student of
Husserl), Thomas Kuhn (a student of Koyré), Imre Lakatos, Mary
Hesse, Stephen Toulmin and Paul Feyerabend.

As Toulmin argues in *Human Understanding,* the attempts of
scientific epistemologies to demonstrate the logical systematicity of
science are contradicted by the history and everyday practice of the
sciences. In a comment which summarizes the character and fate of
the dominant scientific ideology since the seventeenth century,
Toulmin says,

If so much in twentieth-century epistemology lacks an organic connection
with the natural and human sciences, that is not a mark of emancipation
from empirical presuppositions. ... For the questions of twentieth-century
epistemology do still rest on scientific and historical presuppositions. It is
just that these presuppositions are some three hundred years out of date.[3]

Toulmin looks back to the "profoundly original" era of the seventeenth century as a time in which philosophers "did not analyse our
knowledge of the external world by exercises in 'logical construction' alone" and "pieced together conceptions of knowledge from
the best available insights in all related areas of enquiry,"[4] and he
questions the capacity of any contemporary academic discipline to
come to terms with the problem of knowledge:

For the very boundaries between different academic disciplines are themselves a consequence of the current divisions of intellectual authority, and
the justice of those divisions itself one of the chief questions to be faced
afresh.[5]

The starting point of Toulmin's attempt to arrive at a new conception of human understanding is the recognition, on a historical basis,
that "the intellectual content of an entire science normally lacks the
unitary structure characteristic of any single theoretical calculus
employed within that science...."[6] One obvious consequence of this
view is that the notion of a rigorously logical or mathematical
thought – science thinking itself – must be rejected for extended
scientific enterprises. (Schopenhauer, writing before 1820, suggested
as much when he argued,

To desire to make practical use of logic means ... to desire to derive with
unspeakable trouble, from general rules, that which is immediately known
with the greatest certainty in the particular case. It is just as if a man were to
consult mechanics as to the motion of his body, and physiology as to his
digestion.[7])

Mary Hesse and other writers have come at this problem of what
constitutes 'scientific thought' in yet another way, by questioning the
use of models and analogies in scientific practice. Defenders of the
logical systematicity of the hard sciences have doubted, in some
cases, that such aids were strictly necessary. Models and analogies
are, according to Hesse, not only necessary but central to the thinking process in scientific practice: "... if we were forbidden to talk in
terms of models at all, we should have no expectations at all, and we
should be imprisoned forever inside the range of our existing experiments."[8]

    Such criticisms of scientific ideology confirm the appropriateness
of the phenomenological enterprise when it looks for the root character of human knowledge in a situated, intersubjective and historical experience – which is the condition and ground of the sciences
among other things. Yet, so far as a phenomenological criticism is
concerned, the most vital line of twentieth-century phenomenology
only partially came to terms with imagination, at least until
Merleau-Ponty's rethinking of Husserl in his last work.
    Edmund Husserl's phenomenology was concerned to indicate an
epistemological basis for logic, mathematics and hard science in

experience. (He studied mathematics and physics before settling on philosophy as his primary area of endeavor.) The important thing for much of Husserl's work was to find a subjective correlative science; to the extent that this correlative had to reflect the presumed rigor of science, including logic and mathematics, it was natural that the emphasis of his explorations of subjectivity should be upon active consciousness, intentionality, and "eidetic laws." The function of "association," as in Enlightenment thought, is separated out in the analysis of consciousness and described, in the *Cartesian Mediations,* as the "universal principle of *passive* genesis." Husserl acknowledged a "stream of subjective processes"[9] grounding subjectivity but was primarily concerned with how an "objective world" could arise, given such a ground. Characteristically for this approach, language as gesture is not a major topic of Husserl's work, and the exemplary objects of intentionality in his arguments are just that – abstract objects which bear little relation to the manifold existence of things in their experiential contexts.

Husserl's most important contribution, then, to a phenomenology of imagination (and to a phenomenological criticism) was a ground-clearing examination of the epistemological foundations of logic, mathematics, and the sciences, an examination which developed with increasing comprehensiveness and originality throughout his career until, by the time of *The Crisis of the European Sciences* (1934-1937), he confronted the necessity, for a phenomenological epistemology, of an examination of his subject matter in historical and cultural terms.

For Heidegger, a doctoral student of Husserl's in the 1920s, the phenomenology of specific situated expressions was more important than it was for Husserl, but so far as imagination is concerned, it is necessary both to locate Heidegger's philosophical terminology within a systematic metaphysics (so as to be able to translate its possible contents) and to cope with the fact that all of Heidegger's thought proceeds *sub specie aeternitas.* Language, for example, may be identified as living process ("Language speaks."[10]) and, in the authentic work of poetry, as something which "turns our unprotected being into the Open."[11] ("Objectification ... blocks us off against the Open."[12]) But because, for Heidegger, language is above the temporality of human "activity" and "expression," it is necessary to consider it from the otherworldly standpoint of "fundamental ontology." Such an approach radically unsuits this and other segments of Heidegger's thought for the giving of many clues as to a possible phenomenology of imagination. In this regard Heidegger's most interesting contribution would seem to be his examination of Kant's first *Critique* and of the problem of imagination there.

Kant and the Problem of Metaphysics is an exposition of the idea that, in the first edition of the *Critique of Pure Reason,* Kant's grounding of thinking in the transcendental imagination threatened to undo the supremacy of reason itself. Kant drew back from so drastic a reversal of the emphases of his metaphysics of reason. Heidegger is valuable in helping us to understand just how profound was the abyss before which the Enlightenment philosopher stood when, having gone to the very centre of the problem of knowledge, he found an answer which threatened the *ideality* of reason, its separateness from experience, and therefore that metaphysical science of human knowledge and conduct which might spring from it.

However having gone so far in a rereading of Kant, Heidegger does not stop with the problem of imagination but immediately converts it into something else: "The interpretation of the transcendental imagination as a root ... leads naturally back to that in which this root is rooted, primordial times."[13] And so Heidegger's examination of Kant becomes a coda to *Sein und Zeit* rather than the beginning of an exploration of imagination.

If a title could be a sufficient indication, Sartre's *Psychology of Imagination* would seem to have been the work that broke the ground for a phenomenological criticism. Unfortunately, Sartre was too much the student of Husserl and Heidegger for that. "Imagination" for Sartre has to do with the summoning of images rather than with the synthesis which is the flow of experience. For the basis of thinking, Sartre looked to a phenomenology of consciousness which was mathetical in its development of object-relations and image-relations to the thinking subject, which dealt unconvincingly with questions of intersubjectivity, and which, so far as the topic of imagination was concerned, was pre-Kantian in its approach.

The arguments of *Psychology of Imagination,* given the consciousness which Sartre premises, move on inevitably to considerations of the imaginary and the illusory. Sartre:

We have seen that the act of imagination is a magical one. It is an incantation destined to produce the object of one's thought, the thing one desires, in a manner that one can take possession of it. In that act there is always something of the imperious and the infantile, a refusal to take distance or difficulties into account.[14]

The problem here is that imagination is reduced to an act, to the act of positing an image, having an imagery with the sort of clearcut locus in consciousness which a faculty psychology would require. This underpins the received idea that the image is kin to the imaginary, a debased knowledge. Sartre's conclusions about the "relation of imaging to perception," like the conclusions of Merleau-Ponty and Collingwood in their phenomenological criticisms, are drawn from painting, as well as from the schematic drawings which have long been a cliché in experimental psychology. It is really rather strange, and an indication of his commitment to the authority of a reasoning, choosing consciousness, that Sartre the writer did not consider basing this discussion on the phenomenology of literary and dramatic creation.

Sartre's positive contribution is, I think, the idea that the image (after-imagery, hypnagogic imagery, eidetic imagery etc.[15]) is a structure of knowledge:

... knowledge does not disappear once the consciousness of the image is established; it is not 'effaced' behind images. It is not 'always capable of realizing itself as images but always distinct from them.' It represents the active structure of the imaginative consciousness.[16]

This at least signifies that we must not suppose that the interpretation of a poem or novel stops with the 'imagery' offered by the text in so many unit-symbols; rather, as someone has said, we need a field theory of meaning so that more is allowed to the work and to our response than a point theory of meaning permits.

The image as a structure of knowledge, as an intentional structure, has a life of its own, Sartre admits. There is a tension, in fact, between the image which may be left "to develop in accordance with its own law" and the ego which is "free" to vary elements of the image and is never satisfied with it.[17] The activity of this passive thing, the image, while thought is looking the other way, opens up a division and a paradox in "consciousness" which is clearly troubling to Sartre. "The image ... carries within itself a persuasive power which is spurious and which comes from the ambiguity of its nature."[18]

Although R.G. Collingwood's The Principles of Art does not refer

to Husserl or, for that matter, to any of the other names associated
with the development of phenomenology, it is very close to some
lines of analysis in the early work of Sartre and Merleau-Ponty. Collingwood, for example, anticipates Merleau-Ponty's exposition of
language as gesture: "... every kind or order of language (speech, gesture, and so forth) was an offshoot from an original language of total
bodily gesture."[19] His description of the denial of experience, the
"corruption of consciousness," anticipates argument in *Being and
Nothingness*:

> The untruthful consciousness, in disowning certain features of its own
> experience, is not making a bona fide mistake, for its faith is not good; it is
> shirking something which its business is to face. But it is not concealing the
> truth, for there is no truth which it knows and is concealing.[20]

The approach to art through intentionality, situation and gesture
marks *The Principles of Art* as a phenomenological work – that is, as
belonging to a particular style of thought with that label, even if Collingwood doesn't use the label.

There are a couple of respects in which Collingwood's description
of imagination seems to be preferable to Sartre's. He does not argue,
as Sartre does, that imagination is inherently a kind of neutral being
or non-being:

> Sensa [the responses of our 'sensuous-emotional nature' as opposed to our
> 'thinking' or 'rational' nature] cannot be divided, by any test whatever, into
> real and imaginary; sensations cannot be divided into real sensations and
> imaginations. ... That which is true or false is thought; and our sensa are
> called real and illusory in so far as we think truly or falsely about them.[21]

However, substantiating the being of imagination in this way has the
drawback that, within Collingwood's view of consciousness, it is
necessary to concede less to the role of imagination in thought. (By
contrast, Sartre was able to admit the image as a structured kind of
knowledge while segregating it from a primary reality.) The fluidity
of imagination in these treatments is paradoxical; something is there
but not there – and, in any case, must be subordinated to a rational,
choosing consciousness.

Another respect in which the treatment of imagination in *The
Principles of Art* is superior to Sartre is that imagining is given fuller
treatment there as a synthesizing process and, to some extent, the

subordination of imagination to "consciousness" is mitigated by the suggestive discussion of imagination as *activity*:

Attention or awareness is a kind of activity different from mere feeling, and presupposing it. ... Practically considered, it is the assertion of ourselves as the owners of our feelings. By this self-assertion we dominate our feelings.... Their brute power over us is thus replaced by our power over them: we become able on the one hand to stand up to them so that they no longer unconditionally determine our conduct, and, on the other to prolong and evoke them at will. From being impressions of sense, they thus become ideas of imagination.[22]

This is an attractive argument from the standpoint of a phenomenological criticism. Focusing on the *power* of imagination, the argument indicates how, in the case of *Billy the Kid,* the imagination can have political significance:

I am here on the edge of sun
that would ignite me
looking out into pitch white
sky and grass overdeveloped to meaninglessness
waiting for enemies' friends or mine

There is nothing in my hands
though every move I would make
getting up slowly walking
on the periphery of black
to where weapons are
is planned by my eye (74-75)

Collingwood's argument also offers an explanation of the kind of self-control and self-expression which it is often asserted the artist seeks or intends in producing the artwork. (Recall Ondaatje's test of the "emotional or psychological rightness" of a work.) From this sort of reasoning stems the cliché that the (overgeneralized) artist *needs* to create because only in creating can the artist confront those experiences which threaten to be overwhelming.

There are some obvious and serious drawbacks to Collingwood's view of imagination. Imagination has been separated from the experiences of the real (or, rather, this 'common sense' distinction has been retained) and subordinated to consciousness. Imagining is seen as a process enabling consciousness to "dominate" the flux of experience, to escape from the "brute power" of "experiences forcing themselves upon us unawares." Imagination is not thought but "resembles feeling in this, that its object is never a plurality of terms with relations between them, but a single indivisible unity."[23] In all this distinction-making, there is a failure to come to terms with the continuity of thinking – the interrelation between body and world – and reality dogma. Consciousness is reborn as the essence which stands above the flux of experience, which underwrites the instrumentalized reality informing the world of "attention" and "rational thinking" and which, to that end, offers its monadic and systematic solutions of the ambiguities which confront it. Consciousness can absorb all the paradoxes of this role because it is not so much a philosophical term as an authority figure comfortably asserting a centuries-old reality (from capitalism and its scientific ideology) which has never quite managed to explain everything, to bring everything together under the purview of method. Imagination is unsuitable to represent 'thinking' in this hierarchy because it cannot be completely controlled by 'thought' nor can it be identified with entirely purposeful links of cause-and-effect. As Garrett says of Billy, "You could never tell how he meant a phrase, whether he was serious or joking." "... his imagination ... was usually pointless and never in control."

Although Maurice Merleau-Ponty's published writings have little to say explicitly about imagination, they represent a sustained discussion of a number of things which are fundamental to a consideration of imagination and to the development of a phenomenological criticism.[24] Moreover, the works offer a model of such criticism, whether dealing with Cezanne's painting or with the texts of Husserl and Sartre. Husserl, in particular, provides a creative impetus for Merleau-Ponty because his persistent search for the essential terms of a phenomenology which would underpin logic, mathematics and the sciences and offer a description of the a priori and phenomenal characteristics of the life-world touched upon a wide range of philosophical issues. In contrast with Heidegger, whose works are a justification of faith linking ego directly to Being through ontological features such as "authenticity" and "the Open," Merleau-Ponty's thought rarely mystifies its central preoccupations or offers a privatized discourse shaped by a closed philosophical method.

Merleau-Ponty offers a foundation for a phenomenological view of imagination in several ways, even if it is necessary to point out certain unresolved difficulties in his arguments:

1. *Criticism of scientific epistemology.* Merleau-Ponty continued the work of Husserl in an incisive criticism of the relation of the sciences to experience. Although Husserl offered important suggestions about the relation between phenomenology and the so-called human sciences (psychology, sociology, anthropology), Merleau-Ponty greatly extended this discussion in books and articles which not only stated the relation in a general, schematic way but also offered applications of phenomenology to specific issues. The so-called hard sciences receive less attention from Merleau-Ponty although in *Signs,* there is a discussion of Einstein as representative of a "classical science" attitude which denies the epistemological importance for science of "subjective" experience.

The difficulty in Merleau-Ponty's approach to science is that he concedes it a unity of historical essence and of methods which it does not in fact possess; the result is that his phenomenology retains at least the form of a naturalistic orientation. When he specifically confronted this problem in one of this last works, he could only offer the possibility that phenomenology would provide a sounder basis for method in the sciences. About the relation of psychology, considered as a science, to phenomenology, Merleau-Ponty argued:

If eidetic [phenomenological] psychology is a reading of the invariable structure of our experience based on examples, the empirical psychology which uses induction is also a reading of the essential structure of a multiplicity of cases. But the cases here are real and not imaginary. After closer examination, the only difference which we find between inductive procedure – so far as it is justifiable and moves toward what is truly essential – and the procedure of eidetic psychology is that the latter applies imaginary variation to its examples, while the former refers to effective variations in considering the different cases that are *actually realized.*[25]

The important thing for Merleau-Ponty was not that the science of psychology should be subordinated to phenomenology but that it should be recognized, on the one hand, that psychology involves "a certain vision of essence" and, on the other, that phenomenological schematism requires "factual experience."[26] Above all, following Husserl's program, "It must be shown that science is possible, that the sciences of man are possible, and that philosophy also is possible. The conflict between systematic philosophy and the advancing knowledge of science must cease."[27]

Merleau-Ponty never came to terms with the social origins and organization of the science professions or, for that matter, with the problematic role of the professional intellectual. For that reason, the circumspection and detachment of his arguments vis-a-vis the "human sciences" may nowadays strike us as a bit odd, particularly since the import of much of his work goes far beyond the unity of philosophy and science envisioned in the quotation above. Incongruously, he held to an ideal of the systematic unity of thought long after he had abandoned any complete certainty in political action. This is why the work in recent history and philosophy of science mentioned earlier has an important complementary role in a reading of Merleau-Ponty, making clearer the import of his phenomenology for the question of imagination.

2. *The body, gesture and intersubjectivity.* Unquestionably, the heart of Merleau-Ponty's philosophy is the study of world, gesture, and intersubjectivity as they inhere in the situation and expression of the body. This is really the source of his critique of scientific thinking, which is rather inadequate on a historical or sociological level but becomes incisive when he is moving in on descriptions of experience which owe their being to the dogmas of science. The scientific object at whatever level – perceptual constancy, the definition of events, logical systematicity – may serve to suppress the bodily character of experience, especially in its origination of meaning through gesture (including language) and in its opacity. "... the fact that formalization is always retrospective proves that it is never otherwise than apparently complete, and the formal thought feeds on the intuitive thought."[28] We recognize the truth of this; perhaps in the context of this discussion it already suggests that imagination may, after all, be the ground of formalization. However, for Merleau-Ponty, the body in its behavior, in its realm of perception, is the source of philosophy, and this orientation, rich in possibilities, derives much – even in terminology – from psychology, surpassing it in its doubt, in its criticism of the *episteme* of the human sciences, and in its *political* commitment to the originative, liberating character of expression, but not fully developing a view of expression which would have called naturalism itself into question.

Nevertheless, Merleau-Ponty's treatment of gesture, intersubjectivity and world, as understood through the body, brings the phenomenological analysis of thought and expression to the brink of rejection of the epistemological primacy of consciousness, reason, understanding etc., all the descriptions of a commanding faculty or rigorous mental process by which method asserts its truth over anarchy – over, among other things, imagination. In his argument, language is gesture; speech is not the sign of thought, it is thought, as is the written word in its writing:

... it is less the case that the sense of a literary work is provided by the common property of words, than that it contributes to changing the accepted meaning. There is thus, either in the person who listens or reads, or in the one who speaks or writes, a *thought in speech* the existence of which is unsuspected by intellectualism.[29]

The essence of this view of language as originative gesture is summed up in the sentence: "The spoken word is a gesture, and its meaning, a world."[30] But this does not refer to a certain naive conception of language which is rather popular with writers; it does not mean that there is an essentially private or personal creativity in language which originates meaning in a private or personal world. (This particular affectation seems to permeate much of the reviewing and criticism of Ondaatje's work, the critics' atomized view of persons and motives responding unashamedly to Ondaatje's emphasis on the personal without bothering to look into its contradictions.) Language, for Merleau-Ponty, is essentially intersubjective – with other gesture, the ground and meaning of our intersubjectivity. Where speech is concerned, "Available meanings, in other words former acts of expression, establish between speaking subjects a common world, to which the words being actually uttered in their novelty refer as does the gesture to the perceptible world."[31] As to literary language, it is significant that one of Merleau-Ponty's most pointed statements about it was made in the course of a political criticism of Sartre, "Sartre and Ultrabolshevism."

Sartre is criticized for not taking up the social, intersubjective character of literature:

It has not been sufficiently noted that at the very moment when he appeared to take up the Marxist idea of a social criterion of literature, Sartre did it in terms which are his alone and which give to his notion of historicity an absolutely new meaning. In *What Is Literature?* the social is never cause or even motive, it is never behind the work, it does not weigh on it, it gives neither an explanation nor an excuse for it. Social reality is in front of the writer like the milieu or like a dimension of his line of sight.[32]

In *Nausea,* Sartre "became famous by describing a middle ground, as heavy as things and fascinating for consciousness, between consciousness and things," but there is, for Sartre, only "a social field onto which all consciousnesses open" and it is "in front of them, not prior to them, that its unity is made."[33] The expression of the literary work is, however, gestural, founded in the social character of signs and describing its intersubjectivity in the movement toward meaning. The "originality" and "creativity" of the literary work becomes problematic, in this view, only if we forget that there is a level of intersubjectivity, of the synthesis of experience, prior to explicit instrumental or literary constructions. Imagination, considered as a process which is multi-dimensional (non-instrumental) and yet which takes its shape from specific patterns of gesture (instrumental, literary, etc.), can help to avoid any hard-and-fast ontological splitting of expression along levels of prior and explicit meanings.

It should be pointed out that, if Merleau-Ponty's view of the intersubjectivity of language is illuminating for a phenomenological criticism, his understanding of literature's cultural place was stereotyped; unfortunately, Merleau-Ponty was not himself a novelist:

Sartre's permanent revolution, whether effected by the Party or by literature [this was written in the early 1950s], is always a relationship of consciousness to consciousness, and it always excludes that minimum of relaxation that guarantees the Marxist claim to truth and to historical politics. A Marxist does not expect literature to be the consciousness of the revolution, and this is exactly why he will not admit in principle that it be made a means of action. ... Writers are writers: they are persons of speech and experience; one should not ask them to think "objectively" the historical totality. Trotsky said, and Lukács more or less agrees, that it is enough for them to have their honor as writers, and whatever they say, even what is tendentious, is recoverable for the revolution. Ultimately the writer's ideas are of little importance.[34]

I would not disagree with the suggestion here that literature should not be considered a political tool, but Merleau-Ponty is saying much more than that. If the writer's ideas are "of little importance," it is because there are other kinds of knowledge which take priority, and the resurrection of this view of literature as a kind of oblique or secondhand truth, significantly, requires the admission of the dubious qualifier *objectively*, even if it is bracketed. The stereotyping continues in the argument following the quoted passage, Merleau-Ponty (in the manner of Lukács) adducing the reactionary politics and yet revealing literature of Balzac. Might not the "most informed" political actors on the left show similar unevenness in the development of political imagination, yet in a way more likely to be masked by the direction of the movements to which they are committed? This is not to say that political action can be entirely clear in its purposes (Merleau-Ponty defends the necessity of commitment to political action, which is never completely unambiguous or certain in its outcomes) but to make the point that, with the cultural stereotyping of literature, the phenomenological analysis breaks down.

3. *The problem of consciousness; the chiasm.* The precise nature of the relation between consciousness (what Husserl called "active consciousness") and the perceptual, situated, intersubjective ground of consciousness is an issue throughout Merleau-Ponty's work. He marked off, implicitly, the significance of what he was attempting in this regard when he stated the orientation of Husserl and Sartre to the problem:

For [Sartre] ... consciousness, which is constitution, does not find a system of already-present meanings in what it constitutes; it constructs or creates. ... Husserl sees even in this praxis an ultimate problem: even though consciousness constructs, it is conscious of making explicit something anterior to itself, it continues a movement begun in experience, 'It is voiceless experience, which must be brought to the pure expression of its own meaning.' Thence the 'teleology' (in quotation marks) of consciousness, which led Husserl to the threshold of dialectical philosophy, and of which Sartre does not want to hear....[35]

But, given the rejection of a freely choosing, system-making executive consciousness which is somehow (at least potentially) independent of the non-instrumental levels of experience, how does a "voiceless experience" transcend itself to become consciousness? In the early 1950s, Merleau-Ponty's answer was, apparently, the dialectic:

There is dialectic only in that type of being in which a junction of subjects occurs, being which is not only a spectacle that each subject presents to itself for its own benefit but which is rather their common residence, the place of their exchange and of their reciprocal interpretation. The dialectic ... provides the global and primordial cohesion of a field of experience wherein each element opens onto the others. It is always conceived as the expression or truth of an experience in which the commerce of subjects with one another and with being was previously instituted. It is a thought which does not constitute the whole but which is situated in it.[36]

As attribute follows attribute in rapid succession here, it is evident that we are being given the necessary conditions of the dialectic without being told concretely how we live within it. Is the dialectic a fundamental process and, if so, how is it possible for there to be an experience which is undialectical? In effect, Merleau-Ponty's dialectic is only a metaphysical placeholder at the end point of a certain analysis of consciousness. Indicating the difficulty of the questions to be resolved, the term persists into his last work, *The Visible and the Invisible,* and its artificial character is even more apparent there in its derivatives, hyperdialectic ("good dialectic") and bad dialectic. In wishing to establish the explanatory richness of the concept, Merleau-Ponty only confirms its poverty:

... the dialectic is unstable (in the sense that the chemists give to the word), it is even essentially and by definition unstable, so that it has never been able to formulate itself into theses without denaturing itself, and because if one wishes to maintain its spirit it is perhaps necessary to not even name it.[37]

The dialectical relation between "voiceless expression" or "Being" and "consciousness" is not finally a convincing paradox but a mystification of the problem. It is one thing to assert that

One of the tasks of the dialectic, as a situational thought, a thought in contact with being, is to shake off the false evidences, to denounce the significations cut off from the experience of being, emptied – and to criticize itself in the measure that it itself becomes one of them.[38]

And it is quite another to indicate how the dynamic of experience gives rise to the conflict and the criticism necessary for a rejection or bracketing of some part of itself. The word *tasks,* in fact, reveals the imposition of the concept of dialectic upon the process which Merleau-Ponty would describe.

That Merleau-Ponty was uneasy with the "consciousness" which the dialectic was, in part, meant to rationalize is evident from the "Working Notes" which belonged to the genesis of the unfinished text of *The Visible and the Invisible* and which have been appended to the English translation of that work. The overthrow of consciousness by the intervention of a non-objectifying experience threatens "irrationalism" but

One does not get out of the rationalism-irrationalism dilemma as long as one thinks 'consciousness' and 'acts' – The decisive step is to recognize that in fact a consciousness is intentionality without acts, *fungierende* [functioning], that the 'objects' of consciousness themselves are not something positive *in front of* us, but nuclei of signification about which the transcendental life pivots, specified voids....[39]

Here, in an argument which is merely an outline, is indeed the
suggestion of a decisive step. Whatever his concerns about irrationalism, about the truth of science, Merleau-Ponty dissolved the field of
an executive consciousness, of reason and systematicity, into "nuclei
of signification" which are no longer dominant (in his "reform of
consciousness") to "affectivity":

We must no longer ask why we have *affections* in addition to 'representative
sensations,' since the representative sensation also ... is affection, being a
presence to the world through the body and to the body through the world,
being *flesh,* and language is also. Reason too is *in* this horizon – promiscuity
with Being and the world.[40]

Thus, the order of experience, which placed an instrumental thought
at the apex of its hierarchy and authorized the repression of imagination, caves in; there is no longer a consciousness, a reason, an understanding to which it is possible to point in indicating the why and
wherefore of knowledge and of the processes (including the arts) by
which the artifacts of knowledge are produced. Two months after
the above quoted text was written, Merleau-Ponty added:

It is necessary to take as primary, not the consciousness and its
Ablaufsphänomen [concomitant phenomena] with its distinct intentional
threads, but the vortex which this *Ablaufsphänomen* schematizes, the
spatializing-temporalizing vortex (which is flesh and not consciousness fac-
ing a noema)[41]

Here the argument has shifted away from consciousness, even the
"reform of consciousness," altogether, and, interestingly, the shift
has been dictated by the problematic nature of the past – of memory.
    In the last of the "Working Notes," written shortly before his
death, he took up anew the question of the relation of dream and the
imaginary to the real:

Dream. The *other stage* [theatre] of the dream –
    Incomprehensible in a philosophy that adds the imaginary to the real –
for then there will remain the problem of understanding how all that belongs
to the same consciousness – understand the dream starting from the body: as
being in the world without a body, without 'observation,' or rather with an
imaginary body without weight.[42]

The stalemate in thought is almost palpable here. A return to "consciousness," raising the spectre of a unity which cannot hold operational intention and the uncontrolled intention of dream, and then a

reminder to himself to anchor discussion in the body, yet in an "imaginary body." And, later in the same passage, doubt about how the chiasm, the interpretation of body and the world, exists in dream. In search of fundamental terms, ontological terms, the argument is deadended.

Yet, if Merleau-Ponty seems to have led us to the brink of a thought which does not involve the subordination of feeling and the repression of imagination without altogether embracing the consequences in view, he produced a new concept in philosophy, the chiasm, which does suggest (at least in view of other arguments) the unity of real and imaginary in imagination. The chiasm may be seen to be, in fact, a characterization of the way in which bodily experience of the real is an imaginative process:

The chiasm, reversibility, is the idea that every perception is doubled with a counter-perception ..., is an act with two faces, one no longer knows who speaks and who listens. Speaking-listening, seeing-being seen, perceiving-being perceived circularity (it is because of it that it seems to us that perception forms itself *in the things themselves*)[43]

It is clear that this offers a more fundamental view (than, say, classical association) of the way in which, on a continuum, the world is embodied in the subject. Combined with Merleau-Ponty's argument that our meaning-relation to situation is gestural, the concept of chiasm presents subjective experience of the real as a dynamic process which differs from other processes more readily associated with imagination only in the nature of the resistances shaping the subject-world reality. There is a small measure of irony in Merleau-Ponty's ascribing the fullest realization of this dynamic to a novelist:

We touch here the most difficult point, that is, the bond between the flesh and the idea, between the visible and the interior armature which it manifests and which it conceals. No one has gone further than Proust in fixing the relations between the visible and the invisible, in describing an idea that is not the contrary of the sensible, that is its lining and depth.[44]

*

It is beyond the scope of this study to fully develop arguments in support of the view of imagination adumbrated in the preceding. Instead, I have attempted to condense this view of imagination and some of its consequences in a series of theses. Hopefully, the discussion to this point will indicate at least the general shape of the arguments which might be produced in support of these points:

1. Imagination is a complex life process, encompassing the things we normally tag *consciousness, thinking, reason, intuition* and *feeling* as well as dream states. This process is experienced as continuous and multidimensional.[A]

2. The process of imagination takes form through language and other bodily gesture. It is therefore not random in character but structured by the meaning and intersubjectivity inherent in gesture. A patronizing or pejorative description of imagination as, say, "free," or "fanciful," or "anarchic" often essentially misjudges its multidimensional activity by the standards of an instrumental view of thinking.

3. The expressive use of signs is necessarily gestural even in mathematical or logical arguments. So-called abstract thinking must be related expressively to particular styles of experience. We are therefore helped to an experience of mathematical or logical arguments through a style of instruction and social example; without such gestural additions to the repertoire of imagination, learning would be impossible.

4. If instruction is successful in imposing abstract or irrelevant material, what is learned is a style of learning which imposes upon imagination certain deadended, empty or circular patterns of expression. The effective meaningfulness of each moment of imagination may be negated by a line or lines of thought which are essentially empty and therefore destructive of experiencing as such. (Although

A It would be a mistake to psychologize description of the imaginative process – that is, to attempt to translate this process into psychological terms. Although certain results or observations from psychology can offer corroboration or useful points of reference, the scientific underpinnings of psychological discourse are linked to a range of problems within modernism (these are briefly reviewed in Chapter 7). To approach imagination within a particular style of psychological discourse would be, quite possibly, to diminish the importance of the historical study both of imagination itself and of various psychological accounts of it. As well, there are characteristics of thinking about imagination which suggest that a psychological approach would be inappropriate. These characteristics stem from imagination's role as what R.G. Collingwood (in *An Essay on Philosophical Method*) termed a "philosophical concept." Philosophical concepts are not wholly defined, *ad hoc* terms but are terms about which most people have at least some rudimentary knowledge and whose definitions are essentially discursive. Because philosophical concepts require definition by "extended and reasoned" statement, a whole range of definitions is possible – what Collingwood called a "scale of forms" – and these are part of a developing or degenerating historical process of definition. It seems to me that this approach to imagination is likely to be the most fruitful one.

imagination includes both the imposed gesture and the possibility of authentic experience, I have referred to this process as repression of imagination since the decision-making, critical and creative scope of imagination can be straitjacketed.)

5. In the absence of alternative experiences or under the duress of surprise or terror, imagination may return repeatedly to a limited range of intentions or to an objectless flight from situation (such as is experienced in sensory deprivation experiments). The prolonged unfreedom of such imagination is painful rather than the sensual indulgence we might expect from Romantic aesthetics. Intention and choice are essential to imagination as a life process and, in fact, suggest why this ready assimilation and continuous comparison of moments of experience is a life process and the source of issues in a politics of experience.

6. The concept of chiasm (Merleau-Ponty) indicates the way in which the presence of a real situation is assimilated to the flow of imagination, involving (at a complex level of imagination) an intention by which, simultaneously, subject is subsumed in situation and situation is subsumed in subject.

7. If the expressive use of signs is understood as gestural and if gestures are understood as, in some sense, bodily images which carry their situations with them in imagination, then Bruno is right: to think is to think in images.

8. The liberating character of imagination follows from the fact that our imaginations develop through the gestures of others. In gesture, the adult already suggests to the child a fully human equivalent, no matter how the adult may attempt to bracket language or to force an inequality of privilege. On a more sinister level of authority, the oppressor presents, through the intersubjectivity of gesture, a human alternative to the oppressed, which at worst results in the incorporation of the oppressor's vision in the oppressed but, in any case, undermines that vision by suggesting the possibility of a different experience.

9. Because action narrates itself, narrative (or situating) language is the sufficient sign of action. Literary narrative does not simply give a reconstruction of action or situation, therefore, but often conveys with immediacy the flow of intention and action which, given the intersubjectivity of gesture, we experience directly as situated, as relating ourselves and the world.

10. Literature, therefore, is a realm in which the liberating force

and the truth of the multidimensional character of experience may be discovered, and, in a phenomenological criticism, it is important not to second-guess that richness, so close to the basic and unavoidable terms of our humanity, in light of some presumed prior structure which lends itself to interpretation: scientific, archetypal, or onto-logical. The full identification of language with gesture, in all its limi-tation and ambiguity, in its historical and political situation, means that there are no absolute words, no absolute objects for criticism.

11. So far as the conventional critical use of *myth* is concerned, the efficacy of literary narrative does not flow from myth but 'precedes' it.[45] It is, in fact, more to the point, in phenomenological criticism, to use *myth* in an early, classical sense, to refer to a narrative which invokes the open and liberating potentials of imagination as opposed to dogmatic or instrumental purposes.

*

The foregoing discussion of imagination is not meant to imply that Michael Ondaatje has fully realized a philosophical, rather than a technical and intuitive, approach to imagination in his work. The alien world of *The Man with Seven Toes,* the double-bind in Billy's imagination and the character of Billy's pursuer, the music which goes beyond consciousness but also beyond sanity in *Coming Through Slaughter* – these and other tensions in Ondaatje's work indicate that the crisis of imagination is being worked out not from outside, or above, but from within and that, so far as there is an identification between writer and characters, Ondaatje writes out of the experience of imagination chained by imagination. If this is correct, it is somewhat unfortunate that the books have been read as concerning themselves with the plight of the artist. The fault is not the writer's; not all his characters are artists and the experience of imagination he writes about has, in our culture, a universality which a careful reading of Ondaatje should take into account.

On a technical level, Ondaatje has discovered and developed cer-tain ways of achieving forceful effects through a kind of imagistic writing. That he was not always satisfied with words on the page to carry through these effects, he has admitted in discussing the genesis of *Billy the Kid*: "... with *Billy the Kid* I was trying to make the film I couldn't afford to shoot, in the form of a book."[46] Ondaatje was not, it seems, especially sensitive to the fact that the imaginative processes of the writing – the recognition of the work of imagination resulting from his technical approach – would have been submerged in a film version. For in film, never mind the 'realism' of the photography or the words falling into the bottomless well of vision, the instant, one-way logic of duration is continually reimposed on the imagination, which, in interpretation, moves by reflection upon itself.

Perhaps Ondaatje, then, like other writers before him, has been the beneficiary of literature's uncanny capacity for indicating more than was intended. In reading him, the word *imagination* springs to mind not so much because the poetry represents imagism but because, in pushing the language to a particular limit or end condition of expressiveness, Ondaatje has revealed anew the crisis in imagination and the intriguing unity of the artifact of imagination (the text) with the imagination of reception.

To recapitulate: In many specific instances throughout his poetry, Ondaatje's imagery bears a structural resemblance to the imagery of classical, medieval and renaissance memory systems. The structure of the imagery follows an algorithm akin to the classical rules for memory places and the formation of memory images. But the classical rules derived from a practical experience of what would be vividly recalled and what would not be. This common sense reflection on imagery could be to the point in a philosophy of imagination (Bruno) because, in specifying an algorithm for recall, it had reference not only to certain instances of practical experience but as well to an imaginative process giving those instances their special character.

See the rat in the jelly
steaming dirty hair
frozen, bring it out on a glass tray
split the pie four ways and eat
I took great care cooking this treat for you (*RJ* 31)

It's necessary to be aware, in reading the opening lines of "Rat Jelly" that the individual words as text are not concrete but are quite abstract and then that the arc of meaning which answers to *see* – "See the rat in the jelly / steaming dirty hair/ frozen" – still does not give us any place, any explicit situation from which to conjure up jellied rat. And yet, conjure we do, when a word or words call up overlays of situation in which they are gesture (meaning), when the first lines yield things in active relation, the limits of relation being the indicated "you" and the implicit "I." The language of action narrating itself is the sufficient sign of a world.

The reading process is an imaginative process shaped by a variety of experiences, which differ in their characteristics and intensity from person to person; some of the shaping components of the process (all of which must be interpreted gesturally) are:

—Syntactical and logical permutation of relations among phrases and individual words.

—Manner of attention, routine methods of understanding (good or bad).

—Technical proficiency in reading (familiarity with vocabulary, genre, narrative devices, etc.).

—Repressed possibilities, double-binds, knee-jerk responses.

—The building up of intuitive meaning as the text recalls situation(s) and overlays of situation(s).

—Introjection of elements of present situation, recent past etc., which have an entropic pull away from the words and at times return, startlingly, to meaning or meanings which seem to reveal the intention of the text.

This is not an exhaustive list of the qualities of imagination which may be in play in a reading of the opening lines of a poem; and, in a very important sense, the writer uses the discontinuities in the familiar components of the reading process to send the reader back to the root of meaning, the gesture which unites the richness of a concrete situation in its own movement toward meaning.

But in a culture which represses situation in the instrumentality of its work, its schools, and its media entertainment, the interrogation of experience through the discontinuities of the artwork is not easy; the absurdity is that such interrogation – so important to our creative and potentially liberating sense of daily "making the world" – may not find response in an imagination dominated by empty categories and passive conclusion-making. This is the why of those violent, extravagant "words" in Ondaatje's writing, and why the very creation of imagery from such words involves the imagination doing violence upon the world which represses it and, because it also includes the gestures which make that world, doing violence upon itself. I argued earlier that this double-edged character of the repressed / repressive imagination is fundamental to the character of Billy in *Billy the Kid*. The collected works of Billy the Kid are the end-products of the repressed imagination seeking the reality of its

own experience; Billy's momentary triumphs in this struggle to find a
purely experienced, unambiguous core to his existence – as momentary as a shooting – run on to uncanniness, paranoia, and nightmare,
suggesting the boundary which holds his imagination to its circularity. The solipsism of character is reflected in the self-explanation of
the writer, whose imagination is contained not within Billy's
double-bind of course but within an aesthetic which, in its most vivid
creations, is haunted by the uncertainty of its relation to reality.
Haunted by that uncertainty but also feeding on its rationales. There
is something more here than the writer's perennial or perhaps 'archetypal' condition as an artist.

   This last is a point which is, I think, fundamental to understanding the achievement of Ondaatje's poetry. The artwork is not – not
even potentially – a self-contained, ideal expression; the artist does
not, and cannot, live in some state of grace which is sealed off from or
independent of society. Criticism involving 'myth' or 'archetype'
seems to offer a hinterland to which the artwork can escape from
solipsistic expression, from encapsulated literary imagination. So far
as such criticism offers ideal objects for the imagination, however, it
does not offer anything for the essential struggle, the expression of
the reality of the artist's experience. When looking at the direction of
Ondaatje's work, therefore, it is important to avoid equations such
as: *The Man with Seven Toes* equals myth; *Billy the Kid* equals condition of the artist; *Coming Through Slaughter* equals portrait of the
artist. Whatever critical dogmas emerge in these works is relatively
unimportant (as labelling) beside the fact that, fundamentally, each
work represents an imaginative struggle toward articulation in
which the critical clichés probably represent barriers to expression.
Second-guessing the outcome of his work, Ondaatje himself may be
found on the safe side of the conflicts which the work illuminates.
For example, responding to a question about *The Man with Seven
Toes,* he has said,

It had to be brief and imagistic because the formal alternative was to write a
long graphic introduction explaining the situation, setting, characters and so
on. All the geographical references in the book are probably wrong and I'm
sure all Australians think the book is geographically ridiculous, just as peo-
pie of the south-west might think *Billy the Kid* is. I was putting geographical
names into the latter cos I liked the sound of them. Chupadero Mesa, Punta
de la Glorieta. The sound of words was something that concrete poetry woke
me up to at that time.[47]

Reading this (from the 1975 *Rune* interview), we might get the idea that only the most narrow formal considerations dictated the choices Ondaatje discusses. But the poem "had to be brief and imagistic" because of certain limitations built into Ondaatje's aestheticism, the same limitations which carried him forward with the idea even though he could not relate it to the geography of Australia. It's not as if narrative poetry encompassing the sort of detail Ondaatje mentions – "explaining the situation, setting, characters" – has not been written. Moreover, it's not that Ondaatje maintained the same view of poetry from *The Man with Seven Toes* to *Billy the Kid* and beyond. If the geography in *Billy the Kid* has phoney names, at least it has names; there is an obvious move in the later work toward feeling the relevance of just those details of environment and history which were never brought into the plan for *The Man with Seven Toes*. (Because of this, Ondaatje could no longer write such a book.) In a few things in *Billy the Kid* and *Rat Jelly* and in the more recent poems "Dashiell" and "Light," he seems to be feeling his way toward a kind of discursive poetry which would permit the image to emerge from a landscape which includes everything. Consider just this portion of "Light":

And this is my Mother with her brother Noel in fancy dress.
They are 7 and 8 years old, a handcoloured photograph,
it is the earliest picture I have. It is the one I love most.
A picture of my kids at Halloween
has the same contact and the same laughter.
My Uncle dying at 68, and my Mother a year later dying at 68.
She told me about his death and the day he died
his eyes clearing out of his illness as if seeing
right through the room the hospital and she said
he saw something so clear and good that his whole body
for that moment became youthful and she remembered
when she sewed badges on his trackshirts.
Her voice joyous in telling me this, and her face light and clear.
(My firefly Grandmother also dying at 68.)[48]

Here Ondaatje is exploring a structure of feeling too diffuse for his spare, imagistic writing, and he is writing in the first-person, without characterization of the "I," about personal history. Without judging this writing over against *Billy the Kid* and the other poetry, it is at least possible to see, from "Light" and "Dashiell," that Ondaatje is aware of other potentials in the art. Interestingly, the directness of expression in these poems is reminiscent of uncollected poems of the Sixties – in particular, "Little Old Man" springs to mind. "Little Old Man" was not a successful poem – the writer's sympathies were too obviously concerned to make something out of emotion, but it indicates a realm of complex everyday experiences which was not especially important in the poetry until the appearance of *Rat Jelly* and the 1975 *Canadian Forum* poems.

Ondaatje's literary imagination has not stayed within the derivative categories of its beginning; it has developed precisely because the conflict in works such as *Billy the Kid* is not just about the condition of the artist or personal vision or the creation of new 'myths' but is, more importantly and from line to line, the imagination's movement – often frustrated – toward its unco-opted, intersubjective and politicized liberation.

Given that *Billy the Kid* arises from the conflicts of the repressed / repressive imagination, with their tacitly intersubjective and therefore political meanings, it is quite mistaken to conclude about the book, as Dennis Lee does in *Savage Fields,* that "Strife is amoral."[49] Lee in fact comes dangerously near to making the vision of the writer coincide with the vision of a character:

So there is no longer any appropriable meaning, within the planet Ondaatje depicts, to 'right and wrong,' 'good and evil,' 'justice,' 'holiness,' 'truth.' There is no explanation of why these things should have lost their meaning.... But in *Billy the Kid* their meaning *has* collapsed. The kind of consciousness which Ondaatje recreates in Billy is simply not capable of sustaining a vision of things which includes justice or goodness as meaningful alternatives.[50]

The explanation of this rather confusing argument is that Lee is looking for certain absolutes which are not there. What, then, does he make of the structure of reflection and choice throughout the work? The problem is that Lee's metaphysical terms of analysis do not permit him to see that the world of *Billy the Kid* is a moral world, of social and political conflicts and polarities (most often within Billy himself), even if it is a world which is beyond conventional or dogmatic morality. Drawing upon Heidegger, Lee is closer to the theologian than to the phenomenologist. The translated work from which Lee has taken the opposition "earth" and "world" (modifying it for his purposes) is *Poetry, Language, Thought,* about which I have argued elsewhere,

> For Heidegger's discussion of poetry, history is co-essential with truth, and in certain passages of *Poetry, Language, Thought,* he presents some rather concrete notions about the historicity of poetry. Yet it is far more important that he doesn't deal with poetry primarily in cultural terms or in terms of the history of a human community.
>
> .....
>
> The theological character of the arguments is unmistakable and suggests, as much else in Heidegger does, that if he has absorbed some of the specific insights of phenomenology, he has abandoned the kind of method which makes it a viable mode of thinking.[51]

Lee acknowledges the ideality of Heidegger's approach, its "a-historicity," but if his own criticism is (in his words) "more secular," it is not more concretely historical. Besides imposing certain absolute terms on the reading of Ondaatje, Lee does not bother to question the work vis-a-vis the floating, ideal character of its historical and cultural reference. Thus, Lee chooses to be blind precisely where the writer has not come fully to terms with himself or his subject matter. A phenomenological criticism does not attempt to come to rest in ultimate terms, but accepts that (after W.C. Fields) language is full of loopholes. The description that fits today will have to be elaborated or discarded in time, and the sense of its major terms may well undergo shifts in meaning. The meaning of any particular expression must not only be tested within the whole of the work but in view of the historical and cultural situation in which the work is produced. The significance of Lee's terms *earth* and *world,* in their applications in *Savage Fields,* does not bear sufficient evidence of such testing; it may be that the result of such re-examination would not be to jettison this opposition, which to some extent demonstrates its fruitfulness in the work, but to return the words to situation, to the politics of experience. Perhaps Lee is already undertaking this, for he remarks near the end of *Savage Fields,* "Clear thought is an achievement of difficult beauty. Yet it cannot finally be good to go on thinking within the models that rule in our civilization...."[52]

If the explicit and startling images of the poetry compel us to think imagery in order to understand imagery, they drive us back upon resources which much in our educations and our working lives has obscured. Alan Richardson's *Mental Imagery* discusses psychological studies which have shown a decline in eidetic imagery between ages 10 and 19; cross-cultural studies indicate that some non-Western societies have greater capacity to experience eidetic images than, apparently, we do.[53] The evidence is sketchy and, at best, merely symptomatic of the problem of imagination. But it helps to make the point that a poetry which compels attention to the image, especially when that image is duplicitous and shaped by conflict as it usually is in Ondaatje, necessitates that in some way the reader should take up the problem of finding a root imaginative experience which is at the source of the round of repressed / repressive imagination. Ondaatje offers an immediate way, the only way to this root imaginative experience, by originating much of what happens in the poetry explicitly in the body or in the senses.

The end of it, lying at the wall
the bullet itch frozen in my head

my right arm is through the window pane
and the cut veins awake me
so I can watch inside and through the window

Garrett's voice going Billy Billy
and the other two dancing circles
saying we got him we got him the little shrunk bugger (BK 95)

The death of Billy is only one of the most impressive examples of the reference of the poetry to the body, something which is a mark of Ondaatje's best writing from his first book. The precision of such writing not only directs us toward the poem but also toward the experience of our own bodies, which, given the instrumentality of our world, is almost irrelevant except when we are ill or taking exercise but which, in this case, becomes the bridge to the root imaginative experience required by the poetry.

Besides giving a means of understanding what happens in the reception of a particular image, the phenomenological treatment of imagination provides the basis for analyzing what happens "between" the segments of the longer works. Given the atomized development of the imagery in *The Man with Seven Toes*, it is surprising that the continuity of the poetry comes through. This continuity, I would argue, is not a function merely of a logical interrogation of the relation of the parts to the whole but establishes itself on a different imaginative level through the vividness, the carnality and the provocation of the segments of imagery. The only link between (page 24)

In the night shapes swing
spit leaf juice at you
hook and stick to shoulders,
grinned teeth nuzzle, burn
with speckled tongues
then fall away and drop
in water purple as a bladder.

and (page 25)

Three days in swamp
waist deep, still as trees;
things against us
necks throbbing at our feet
could feel them fight
wrapped around each other like worms

Ate by reaching to tree stumps
to pick off, swallow the swamp snails, warm

is the situated, concrete imagery of *reception,* which, in effect, creates its own narrative from the brilliant fragments laid out by Ondaatje. In its way, the sense of participation in the poem's realization can be quite remarkable, but the endpoint of this experience is in the reader's own reflection on imagination, on how it was possible — given few clues — for imagination to think through imagery, originating the lines of intention from the reader's own experience. Something like this happens in the reception of every literary work, of course, but very often the reader finds that a work fills up its own horizon, or rather if the work is apparently sufficient unto itself, if there is no provocation, no need for logical interrogation, the reader disregards the difference between meanings created in reception and the meanings evidently intended by the writer.

In *Billy the Kid,* there is more detail than in *The Man with Seven Toes*; the narrative has been spelled out, and many of the segments are rich enough in themselves to suggest that all has been said — that, apart from an obvious narrative or thematic bridge to other segments, they are rather self-contained works within the work. However, here again, because of Ondaatje's skilful evocation of imaginative experience, the segments overflow their limits, the narratives they create being very much something other than mere narrative structure. Rereading the poetry, the centre of narrative is anywhere, each segment may flow into any other which is held within the same movement of imagination. And the segments flow — again, because of their carnality, duplicity and provocation — not by way of logical reconstruction (though interrogation is part of the imaginative process) but by way of thinking in images. Perhaps the most striking irony of *Billy the Kid* is that which exists between the text and the reader. In reception, the text is both the narrative of imagination undone and a very direct evocation of authentic levels of experience in the reader's own imaginative life.

CHAPTER FIVE

Coming Through Slaughter and Tragic Bathos

IN his monograph on Leonard Cohen, Ondaatje described the language of *Flowers for Hitler* as, finally, "anti-poetic, realistic, blending in with everyday speech so that when read aloud they sound like the words of a demagogue." And he offers the explanation that

... Cohen was really becoming a novelist. The best moments in *Flowers for Hitler,* such as the prose passages or rhetorical wit, would not seem out of place in a novel. The rant in these poems is close to the marvellous diatribes of Breavman or F. [characters in Cohen's novels], and the poems very badly need someone out there to continue the arguments or retaliate. Without a character like F. to link them up, they remain unfinished statements – often brilliant but still one step from art because they have no context and have not been dramatized properly. [1]

This suggests a great deal about Ondaatje's view of the novel and of the objectives of art. It suggests that *Coming Through Slaughter* owes its formal existence to the weight of 'realism' – that Ondaatje may not have been entirely satisfied with the mix of factual account, historical parody, and poetry in *The Collected Works of Billy the Kid.* Ondaatje, in any case, does not detach himself from the values of realism in *Coming Through Slaughter,* even if the realism is technically very low key. Although the writing may seem formalistically novel (Dennis Lee found the book one of those rare works which "extend and revalue the matter of fiction"), it falls into the long tradition in English literature of the "true narrative," except that, as opposed to the demand of the seventeenth century for straightforward accounts with a moral point, the "true narrative" of this century is freighted with a scientific ideology which self-consciously juxtaposes all artworks to an objective, or verifiable, factual reality.

But the reality of *Coming Through Slaughter* is anomalous. It offers more and less than conventional realism. Ondaatje's stricture about writing in Cohen's work which has no context is puzzling beside the missing elements of the novel. As in previous books, he has ostensibly written about a time, a place and a condition which he could not be expected to write about well without more painstaking research than is indicated in the credits. Buddy Bolden was black, apparently risen out of poverty, certainly living in the midst of it, in a segregated, oppressed society at a time which saw the nadir of black-white race relations in the United States. The biographical outline in the "Introduction" should indicate how far removed Ondaatje has been from this kind of life, and yet he approaches Bolden not only on the basis of meagre biographical information but decades after the principal events in what is known of Bolden's life.

In *The Man with Seven Toes* and *Billy the Kid,* Ondaatje fully accepted the consequences of using someone else's history – alien, even meaningless events – for poetic material; the result in both cases was, as I have tried to show, a string of brilliantly focused moments which force upon us, as readers, the necessity of imagination. In the novel, by contrast, he chooses to follow the shape of certain historical clues without changing any major assumptions about his art and, most important, without apparently thinking through history itself.

The comment on *Flowers for Hitler* suggests that characterization or the dramatic interplay of characters is sufficient for the creation of context, and *Coming Through Slaughter* both confirms this point of view and illustrates its limitation. Disturbing as the realities of insanity, alcoholism and prostitution are in the novel, more disturbing – and more fundamental – realities have been all but excluded: racism, poverty, work. Where race is concerned, the references are allusive, tentative; the closest thing to an understanding Ondaatje offers is one of Bolden's 'interior' monologues:

Cricket [Bolden's magazine] was my diary too, and everybody else's. Players picking up women after playing society groups, the easy power of the straight quadrilles. All those names during the four months moving now like waves through a window. So I suppose that was the crazyness I left. Cricket noises and Cricket music for that is what we are when watched by people bigger than us. (CS 113-114)

Although the novel places Bolden in the streets, on the roads, in crowds, there is nothing to suggest that his pain and conflict might come from a consciousness of the oppressions of poverty and racism. Bolden appears to act out of an egoism almost wholly preoccupied with sex, art and the violence arising therefrom. He came from

nowhere, it seemed to contemporaries, to take up his career as jazz
musician, and Ondaatje allows that mysterious boundary between
his background and his fame to stand, one more strategic exclusion
in the novelist's field of vision. Nor does Bolden react to the conditions of poverty around him except in the carefully limited description of the ruined prostitutes. The anguish of this is not permitted to
develop into a true common ground; rather, it is turned back upon
ego and focused there in superficial metaphor:

Women riddled with the pox, remnants of the good life good time ever loving Storyville who, when they are finished there, steal their mattress and with
a sling hang it on their backs and learn to run fast when they see paraders
with a stick. Otherwise they drop the mattress down and take men right
there on the dark pavements, the fat, poor, the sadists who use them to piss in
as often as not because the disease they carry has punched their cunts inside
out, taking anything so long as the quarter is in their hands.
.....
Bellocq showed me pictures he took of them long ago, he burned the results.
... Dear small dead Bellocq. My brain tonight has a mattress strapped to its
back.

 Even with me they step into the white [mist]. They step away from me and
watch me pass, hands in my coat pockets from the cold. Their bodies mur-
dered and my brain suicided. Dormant brain bulb gone crazy. The fetus we
have avoided in us, that career, flushed out like a coffin into the toilets and
into the harbour. (CS 118-119)

The series "the fat, poor, the sadists" is another of those flaws in the
writer's projection of character which crop up throughout the book.
Are the "poor" repulsive? It is sometimes a middle-class reflex to
believe so, but it is hardly plausible that a black of Bolden's time and
place would be so glib.
 One of literature's recurring revelations is that the narrative gesture is the sufficient sign of a world and that, so far as this gesture
conforms to a recognizable human conduct coherent in literary personae, living, engaging characterizations are produced. Thanks to
the manipulative use in pop culture, especially in films and television,
of characters which are obviously false or incomplete, it's not necessary to argue very much over whether our feeling response to a character is in itself any measure of the character's plausibility or reality.
Coming Through Slaughter is not amusement art; but with all
narrative artworks it shares the common ground of narrative and

characterizing gesture with pop literature and dramatic media. In a phenomenological criticism, affecting narrative does not have a privileged status as literature just because it appears in a work with literary pretensions. The problem where reception is concerned is, in fact, to determine how reception is manipulated, how mystification takes place.

The powerful writing in the narrative of the Bolden-Pickett fight gives high definition to the behavior of violent passions. We are drawn into the movement of the writing so fully that we may not even notice the stock treatment of jealousy which provides a structure for the description.

Next time he swings the chair I drop the razor and wrestle it from him and push him backwards now able to keep the strop off but my left hand is still dead. See Nora in another mirror. The parlor is totally empty except for the two of us and Nora shouting in a corner at the back screaming to us that we're crazy we're crazy. (CS 74)

The atoms of distanced descriptive language and the shifts in narrative voice are pulled together in reception, fascinate with their unity of suggestion. Imaginative closure; for there is nothing else, no situation beyond the action, no link in the action itself to suggest how Bolden's character could be understood in real terms.

Bolden's character is at last a solipsism because it lays claim to an existence in the world and yet is posited in a way which denies a real relationship to the world. Everything fed into the imaginative train revolves around an "I" – not an historical ego but a construction from shakey metaphysical premises. (It is not relevant for this argument that the character makes a claim for ego or explains through ego or that Ondaatje produces an explicit connection between himself and the character:

When I [Ondaatje] read he stood in front of mirrors and attacked himself, there was the shock of memory. For I had done that. Stood, and with a razor-blade cut into cheeks and forehead, shaved hair. Defiling people we did not wish to be. [CS 133])

The character is posited independently of those contexts which alone could give grounds for comprehension, the metaphysical assumptions being that art's realm is the personal, concrete moments of observed experience in their immediacy and objectivity and that some of these particulars represent a universal, mythic

level of human experience. It is futile to attempt to find, among the
elements of the narrative, something which 'explains' Bolden, even
something which explains jazz and the jazz artist. (Amiri Baraka,
inveighing against white jazz critics, stated that, in jazz, "The notes
mean something; and the something is, regardless of its stylistic considerations, part of the black psyche as it dictates the various forms
of negro culture."[2])

Not that explanation of Bolden isn't offered. There is, after all, no
point in delivering a history ending in madness if the writer must say
at the end that what happened in the case is a complete mystery. And
so there are explanations:

1. Here. Where I am anonymous and alone in a white room with no history
and no parading. So I can make something unknown in the shape of this
room. Where I am King of Corners. And Robin who drained my body of its
fame when I wanted to find that fear of certainties I had when I first began to
play, back when I was unaware that reputation made the room narrower
and narrower, till you were crawling on your own back, full of your own
echoes, till you were drinking in only your own recycled air.

2. I really wanted to talk about my friends. Nora and Pickett and me. Robin
and Jaelin and me. I saw an awful thing among us. And that was passion
could twist around and choose someone else just like that.
.....
We had no order among ourselves. I wouldn't let myself control the world of
my music because I had no power over anything else that went on around
me, in or around my body. My wife loved Pickett, I think. I loved Robin
Brewitt, I think. We were all exhausted. (CS 99)

Such explanations are necessary because the narrative line generates
no self-evident sense of the way in which Bolden's insanity follows
necessarily from the life preceding it. The explanations may offer
immediate causes which sustain the narrative focus; but as clues to
character seen whole, they lead nowhere, or, to be more precise, they
intersect in a bathetic mystification which ends the serious questioning before it has really begun.

Schiller condemned bathos ad hominem — in humanistic terms
which called into question whether such a sentiment in itself could
have an authentic role in art. Although it is no longer possible for us
to accept (perhaps even to fully understand) the premises of Schiller's
humanism, his criticism of the bathetic seems to have relevance for a

criticism of *Coming Through Slaughter*.^A It may also have relevance generally for a literature which is seen in terms of victims. For the bathetic is a kind of trap into which a one-dimensional treatment of victim's point-of-view may lead. The title of Margaret Atwood's study of victims in Canadian literature is significantly not *Victims* but *Survival*. Perhaps the second "basic victim position" she describes is closest to bathos:

To acknowledge the fact that you are a victim, but to explain this as an act of Fate, the Will of God, the dictates of Biology (in the case of women, for instance), the necessity decreed by History, or Economics, or the Unconscious, or any other large general powerful idea.³

But this does not suggest that a human oppressor – rather than a "large general powerful idea" – may be the cause of a similar victim position, nor does Atwood elsewhere go into the question of whether literary bathos may have an authentic relation to its subject matter or indicates some deficiency in the artwork itself.

In Schiller's view, suffering is not necessarily a fit subject for art; rather, the depiction of suffering may call into question that very freedom in the artwork and in humanity which is one of its reasons for being:

... real taste excludes all extreme affections, which only put sensuousness to the *torture*, without giving the mind any compensation. These affections oppress moral liberty by *pain*, as the others by voluptuousness; consequently they can excite aversion, and not the emotion that would alone be worthy of art. Art ought to charm the mind and give satisfaction to the feeling of moral freedom. This man who is a prey to his pain is to me simply a tortured animate being, and not a man tried by suffering. For a moral resistance to painful affections is already required of man – a resistance which can alone allow the principle of moral freedom, the intelligence, to make itself known in it.⁴

There is, surely, a sense in which the character Buddy Bolden puts "sensuousness to *torture*" in reception. Apart from the sort of explanation which is used here and there to pull the threads of the

---

A I am using *bathos* and *bathetic* in senses which I believe to be logical extensions of their most commonly accepted meaning: that is, a sudden descent from the sophisticated to the commonplace or the banal. Starting from such a core idea, it seems that the definition of *bathos* might logically be extended to include all cases in which character sharply descends from an understood or explicit level of human dignity to passivity and reification. Schiller, of course, did not use *bathos* in this sense but that he understood such an option to exist for the artist will be made clear in the discussion.

narrative together, Bolden is presented more in "pure sensation" – in objectified "feeling" – than in the coherence of imagination. The imagery – violent, passionate, sensual – comes home to us, but it is disturbing more than clarifying. It recalls, and is no doubt related to, the reified savagery of a movie such as "Taxi Driver." The artwork which seemingly has no politics presents a world without freedom, and, whether this condition is articulated or not, it is experienced as – in the most fundamental sense – politically repressive.

Not surprisingly, the bathetic realization of Bolden's "tortured animate being" finds expression in identification with an animal:

The dog follows me wherever I go now. If I am slow walking he runs ahead and waits looking back. If I piss outside he comes to the area, investigates, and pisses in the same place, then scratches earth over it. Once he even came over to the wet spot and covered it up without doing anything himself. Today I watched him carefully and returned the compliment. After he had leaked against a tree I went over, pissed there too, and scuffed my shoes against the earth so he would know I had his system. He was delighted. (CS 90)

This is funny; but it lacks the imaginative tension of, say, Billy's encounters with animals in *Billy the Kid* because, in substance, it is only one more underscoring of the character's drift toward bathetic non-being.

The "moral resistance to painful affections" in *Coming Through Slaughter* is not a dynamic which involves continuous resistance but an episode at the centre of the narrative: Bolden's dropping out of his life as jazz musician and seeking to live entirely within the private triangle of relationships with Jaelin and Robin Brewitt. The suicide Bolden contemplates – "my brain suicided" – is not a final desperate act of liberation but a state of complete passivity. The irony of this passivity is brought home in the passage

He lay there crucified and drunk. Brought his left wrist to his teeth and bit hard and harder for several seconds then lost his nerve. Flopped it back outstretched. Going to sleep while feeling his vein tingling at the near chance it had of almost going free. Ecstasy before death. It marched through him while he slept. (CS 79)

The original of this crucifixion is a symbol of choice, not of withdrawal. Bolden retreats from what would have been at once his self-destruction and an assertion of his freedom. With its descent from the suggestion of ultimate choice to the passivity of mere sensation and sleep, the passage epitomizes the bathetic movement of the novel as a whole.

In Schiller, pathos is the necessary basis of the sublime in art and the "first condition required most strictly in a tragic author." He does not suggest that art should avoid the depiction of suffering or (from the standpoint of the artist's task rather than of taste) the depiction of extremes of suffering.

... resistance can only be measured by the strength of the attack. In order, therefore, that the intelligence may reveal itself in man as a force independent of nature, it is necessary that nature should have first displayed all her power before our eyes. The *sensuous* being must be profoundly and strongly *affected, passion* must be in play, that the *reasonable* being may be able to testify his independence and manifest himself in *action.*[5]

It's unnecessary to accept the dichotomy between ego and the 'external world' or the faculty psychology sense of *reason* to find validity in what Schiller is saying. If an artwork is to lead to a liberating imaginative experience, it must in some fashion embody the tension of the oppositions and oppressions which necessitate resistance and, integrally with that, express those choices which are resistance. And Schiller goes further than this. He would say, I think, that insofar as we are fully human, suffering will lead us to resistance; in a still more general sense, human opposition to a merely contingent world makes the world *human*:

... that he [man] may not only be a world, he must give form to matter, and in order not to be a mere form, he must give reality to the virtuality that he bears in him. He gives matter to form by creating time, and by opposing the immutable to change, the diversity of the world to the eternal unity of the Ego. He gives a form to matter by again suppressing time, by maintaining permanence in change, and by placing the diversity of the world under the unity of the Ego.[6]

This begins to explain why the humanity of the Buddy Bolden characterization is not realized and is even obscured by *Coming Through Slaughter*. "We had no order among ourselves," Bolden says. "I wouldn't let myself control the world of my music because I had no power over anything else that went on around me, in or around my body." In light of Schiller's view of experience – very much a politics of experience, it is possible to see how this statement, in its finality, is bathetic and, in essence, untrue to the nature of suffering.

Resignation, the abasement of ego, withdrawal are never simple acts. An expectation in reading *Coming Through Slaughter* may be that there is another dimension to the bathos, that upon reflection the complete Buddy Bolden will emerge. But Ondaatje offers the contrary – a character which finally disappears among the records of the East Louisiana State Hospital. We are not given a Bolden who wills himself to accept the sterility of the insane asylum, who must struggle against the contrary impulses to liberty and new experience. The mood of Bolden's self-explanation in the cited passage is understandable, as is the mood of other moments in the narrative; but only as transient experience. The once-and-for-all explanatory emphasis – "I had no power" – extends a comprehensible mood into something untrue. For here is a characterization of powerlessness which asserts, by implication, that power was necessary but which offers, in the sequel, a succumbing to powerlessness that sustains no dialectical relationship with the need for power. "We were all exhausted," Bolden concludes. The contradiction is the same in the monologue

Here. Where I am anonymous and alone in a white room with no history and no parading. So I can make something unknown in the shape of this room. Where I am King of Corners. (*CS* 86)

Into the "I can make" slips an affirmation of choice, which is submerged in the methodical reification of existence.

The problem of contradiction and authenticity is twofold: In the first place, Ondaatje is asserting an equivalence between ego and a certain restricted area of experience – art, fame, relations with friends and lovers – an equivalence which may have momentary and approximate truth but which finally does not measure up to the complexity of existence, certainly not to the extent of permitting him to explain a case of insanity. One does not have to be a historian to feel that early experience, race and work must have been more significant in Bolden's story than he suggests.

In the second place, no matter what the nature of the oppression, it is not possible for one to choose not to choose, even suicide or the endless rote rationalizing of suffering being an expression of a humanity which must continually remake its world in order to dwell within it at the level of thought and speech. With the persistence of a writer who harbors a specific formal intention, Ondaatje pushes the character of Bolden into thinghood, into bathetic unbelievability, even when language, as we have seen, moves into contradiction.

Perhaps he sensed as much in the working out of the novel, for he finally offers a cop-out: "Laughing in my room. As you try to explain me I will spit you, yellow, out of my mouth" (CS 140). If this means, on one level, that the character of Bolden is frightening and will provoke attempts at explanation, it misses altogether the sense in which we respond to the character: "This man," as Schiller argued, "who is a prey to his pain is to me simply a tortured animate being, and not a man tried by suffering." Which is to say, in this context and in the different terms I have used here, that we cannot follow a tragic character into bathos, that such a treatment of character leaves behind the evocative reality of human gesture.

But does insanity, that realm of ultimate mysteries, perhaps offer an out? I have indicated that there is a 'tactical' reason why it must not be the final explanation in a historical narrative which turns on the drama of the transition from sanity to insanity. But there is also a strong argument to be taken from psychiatry or, rather, anti-psychiatry. R.D. Laing's work – for example, *The Divided Self* – has urged that so-called insanity is often a bizarre, highly individual, sometimes highly ingenious defence against the "sane" and miserable social environment (the family being a persistent focus of this interaction). "Insanity" then becomes an assertion of "the *inner honesty, freedom, omnipotence,* and *creativity,* which the 'inner' self cherishes as its ideals."[7] Because experience is complex and because narrative very often suggests the imaginative character of that complexity, it is not sufficient demonstration of the novel's shortcomings merely to offer in evidence a work of psychology, with that commonplace presumption that statements in the sciences or in professional disciplines have a first hand relation to truth which literature lacks. But, such prima facie arguments aside, Laing's work does confirm the unreality of Ondaatje's one-dimensional treatment of Bolden.

*

And so it is not clear that Ondaatje was "becoming a novelist" in *Coming Through Slaughter.* The novel is a deceptively free narrative form. Confronted with demands of continuity and characterization, which are often only present by suggestion in poems, the writer must extend the articulation of experience far beyond the everyday limits of anecdote, description and argument. Whereas the shape of a poem, even its full articulation, may be grasped in one sweep of the imagination, the planning and writing of a novel involves an off-again, on-again struggle with details, connections, with building up and paring down, with the selection and rejection of the shape and the possible shape of what is being written. Finally, the novel which presumes to have significance lays out all the attitudes, the thought and the foibles of the artist as no other art form. The imaginative reach of the novel is something which, to an important extent, cannot be defined in the act of writing, the only defence against the betrayal of language being the cohesion and appropriateness of the writer's thought. In precocious novels, such as Marie-Claire Blais' early work, the cohesion and appropriateness of the thought need not entail comprehensiveness; it is enough if the writing consistently and honestly reveals a point-of-view, even a naive point-of-view, without pretensions to something more. Usually, however, the imaginative scope of the novel requires that the cohesion and appropriateness of the novelist's design reflect the imaginative comprehension of experience, giving it an orientation and significance which is multidirectional and accurate.

The highly focused observation, the use of simple and powerful contrasts (animal being versus human consciousness, for example), and even the dialectic between the identity asserted on the page and the writer's detachment are stimulating in Ondaatje's poetry but, extended or elaborated to meet the demands of the novel, are, in this case, insufficient to the form without the imaginative comprehension of the subject matter, in its historical complexity, which would have provided the basis – the orientation and imaginative force – for the development of a fully realized narrative.

CHAPTER SIX

The Films

SIGNIFICANTLY, Michael Ondaatje, by his account, turned to the project of making his first film, "Sons of Captain Poetry," as an escape from literary language:

At that time I was very interested in the possibilities of concrete poetry and I'd just finished the actual writing of *The Collected Works of Billy the Kid* and there was a real sense of words meaning nothing to me anymore, and I was going around interpreting things into words. If I saw a tree I just found myself saying tree: translating everything into words or metaphors. It was a very dangerous thing for me mentally and I didn't want to carry on in that way. I just felt I had to go into another field, something totally visual. The film was quite a help cos it freed me from going around and doing this kind of thing.[1]

The impulse to make a film, for other reasons, had already been there, before the writing of *Billy the Kid*. What Ondaatje seems to be saying here is that, even after completing his greatest literary success, he found literary language to be a trap. The aestheticism of *Billy the Kid* – the distancing, the 'objectivity' of structure, the carefully sustained modes of a language meant to be at once mythic and immediate – involved its own self-conscious 'translation' of the world in the search for a unity of vision. Its studied manner of observation opposed to the in-common world of our everyday intersubjectivity a pattern of transcendence, which was also a pattern of negations, ruling out the everyday sense of the political and the historical, which were not in Ondaatje's view the province of his writing. It's not surprising that a process of composition which enhanced the writer's sense of isolation and inner conflict should have led to the exhaustion of meaning which Ondaatje describes.

Perhaps the best way to understand this exhaustion is to consider the captioning of visual imagery in some of those recent works which purport to convey archetypal ideas – for example, *Seeing with the*

Mind's Eye by Mike and Nancy Samuels. In this work one will find
the photographic image of a wooden ladder leaning against an adobe
building labelled "A striking image of ascent"; a line drawing with
the caption "The meadow is a basic symbol which represents the primordial, creative basis of a person's life and is a natural departure
point for visualizing other symbolic images such as a forest or a
stream"; an oil painting landscape decoded: "The mountain symbol-
izes spiritual elevation. In ascending the mountain a person must
work to overcome obstacles. The mountain can also symbolize a
person's ambition, career, and worldly goals. When a person visual-
izes climbing the mountain inward transformation takes place"; etc.
The metaphysical guarantee of the validity and integrity of our
experience which this labelling and metaphorizing of particulars
involves can be an incredibly liberating and creative thing, over
against the rules and regulations of the instrumentalized world. It
offers one sort of 'objective correlative.' But, finally, it substitutes
symbolic for actual experience; far from reducing the isolation and
unreality of the artist's world, in Raymond Williams' words,

The historically variable problem of "the individual and society" acquires a
sharp and particular definition, in that "society" becomes an abstraction,
and the collective flows only through the most inward channels. Not only the
ordinary experiences of apparent isolation, but a whole range of techniques
of self-isolation are then gathered to sustain the paradoxical experience of an
ultimate collectivity which is beyond and above community.[2]

Such a translation of the world impoverishes experience, channelizes
imagination oppressively, falls into solipsism (since it turns on the
isolation of the subject), and can become a 'dangerous thing,' with
terrors of its own.

   The film image does not directly restore imagination to authenticity so much as it captures, permanently, the 'incidentals' of vision
which aestheticism in literary language would have dispensed with.
And this is surely the source of humor in the opening shots of "Sons
of Captain Poetry" as the camera moves around and within a herd of
dairy cattle while the voices-over launch into the ostensible subject
matter of the film. With the camera at close range, the images of the
cattle defy symbolic constructions — especially those of otherworldly literary preoccupations — and force upon us the details of the
situation itself. If we can get past amusement and intellectual frustration in taking this in, there is at least a clue here to the revitalization

of imagination as well as the obvious connection to certain levels of experience explored in bpNichol's sound poetry.

"Sons of Captain Poetry" is a 35-minute color film, with soundtrack, produced in 1970 by Ondaatje in collaboration with Robert Fresco and with the technical assistance of the Queen's University film department. The film required two weeks of shooting and two months of editing. It is subtitled "a film on bp nichol" and Ondaatje has indicated that, among other motives, there was an important critical intent: "... I had wanted to write something on nichol and I'd realized that you couldn't really *write* about concrete poetry, that it had to be expressed in another form."[3] In fact, as a critical work, the film is rather unique in the Canadian setting because it combines the critic's attempt to make sense of a poetic enterprise with the poet's own selection, utterance and performance for the quiet eye of the camera. This is also the central structural problem of the film as when the poet's talk about his family makes its way (voice-over) against a montage of old photographs or when, less successfully, the poet's reading is voice-over to montages of magazine and comic-strip imagery. The balancing act between the filmmaker's choices and those of the performer is not always exact. The poet throws out a comment (arising from Hugo Ball) about the dangers of performance: "You put the audience into your perceptual system," but the filmmaker does not elaborate and, in fact, we do not see Nichol or the Four Horsemen in performance before an audience.

On the other hand, when Nichol talks about the survival technique of becoming a master of as many different levels of perception as possible ("survival technique" because, he points out, the world insists on *one* level of perception), there is an unmistakable identity of purpose between filmmaker and poet. The moment serves to pull together the readings, the performances of Nichol and the Four Horsemen for the camera, and the 'concrete poetry' of letters in address and commercial signs, the comic-strip and pop-art imagery, the recollections of the photo album. As well, it indicates, if obliquely, Nichol's Therafields experience and suggests the motive behind those other moments in the film when Ondaatje attempts overt political statement.

The weakness of the film's critique of perception, through Nichol's poetic vision, is that it does not, well and consistently, explore the political character – the politics of experience – in this vision. Early on, it presents the poetry wearing the mask of bourgeois literature – "fast, kitschy, funky, built-in obsolescence" – and the poet wearing the mask of the bourgeois writer – "barrie's poetry has no greater chance than anyone else's" – while Nichol himself directs us to a quite different understanding of the values involved in his work.

Without the inspiration of an essentially political view of Nichol's work, Ondaatje leaves some of the important questions unasked. For example, the sound poetry offers involvement, even a community of purpose, to its audience, yet it is obviously limited in its collective realization by certain conditions of performance and reception in our culture; does Nichol recognize the problem, have a strategy of composition and performance to cope with it? The film really doesn't supply the answer. The overt politics of the film, so far as the filmmaker's choices are concerned, seems symbolic and inconsequential. The montages of pop art are merely camp rather than explosive; capitalist greed jumps out of a comic strip by Winsor McCay but goes nowhere as subject matter. Apart from the deserted warehouse symbol (perhaps), the landscapes of the film – much countryside from a car window – do not move very far beyond that contact with the non-literary real which Ondaatje was seeking. Particularly unfortunate is that Nichol's most direct political statement of the film – the chant

you are city hall my people
look what you've done
you are city hall my people
look what you've become

– comes off as out-of-context or demagogic.

The Therafields experience, touched upon late in the film, might have offered a way of clarifying the political import of the poetry. Based on the work of radical psychiatry, the Toronto-based Therafields group developed a program of therapy in the late Sixties to "truly see the history of the family as the transmission of unresolved neuroses from generation to generation." A 1973 article in *Canadian Forum,* of which Nichol was one of the writers, pointed out, "Only the anarchist tradition in politics has hinted at something similar [to this critique of the family], but only as an idea."[4] Although the focus of Therafields was the family rather than politics in the narrow sense, the analysis in therapy was intended to develop a politics of experience. That Nichol's sense of this politics does not fully emerge in the film, therefore, constitutes a rather serious defect in Ondaatje's handling of his critical task.

Ondaatje's next film was "Carry on Crime and Punishment," produced in 1972. Not much needs to be said about it. It is a few minutes in length, with a storyline about the theft and recovery (by a mass of children) of the Ondaatjes' hound, and comes off as perhaps the most technically exact home movie ever shot in Canada. Clearly the filmmaker was keeping his hand in, working at the fundamentals.

In 1974, with assistance in cinematography from Robert Carney and Robert Fresco, Ondaatje filmed "The Clinton Special," in length (70 minutes) and subject matter a more ambitious film than "Sons of Captain Poetry." And yet "The Clinton Special" does share some of the characteristics of the earlier film. The movie camera is again directed toward an open-ended experience, an *observed* experience, the instrumental eye framing and representing the possibilities of vision. This fascination again moves, self-consciously, beyond the limits of Ondaatje's literary aestheticism. About one aspect of this he has said,

I just became really fascinated with *the way* that people talk, not just what they're saying, but the way they kind of choose a word or think it up. Something that people like Ray Bird – the fellow who gave the company the barn – did; he would really think out, and think out on film. That was a nice element I wanted to save.[5]

The camera, under Ondaatje's direction, does not move around to create a sense of action, but observes, often faithfully capturing the gestures and expressions of the social relations which are the core of the film. But, as in "Sons of Captain Poetry," the camera's subject is occasionally discovered to be in dialogue with Ondaatje, the filmmaker outside the movie frame, and this can be disturbing, even when the subject is an actor and supposedly capable of working within such an artificial limit.

Also, like the earlier film, "The Clinton Special" is, in important respects, a work of criticism, exploring the nature of an important experiment in theatre and, inevitably, through the selection and shaping of what it records, evaluating. At times, the sheer vitality of the Theatre Passe Muraille carries the film in directions which run counter to the emphasis-by-editing Ondaatje tries to give. The balancing act between the intentions of the filmmaker-critic and the drive of performance is, if anything, even more difficult than in "Sons of Captain Poetry." To Ondaatje's credit, he neither lets the Passe Muraille company take over the film, supplying all its energies, nor imposes himself on each moment of expression as relentlessly as in the Nichol film. This is not to say that there are no wrong turns in the film. There are moments which seem to have been especially troublesome. To place them within the film however, it's first necessary to give some background.

"The Clinton Special" is not primarily a record of Theatre Passe Muraille's performance of *The Farm Show* but a documentary study of the sources, the development and the artistic problems of this performance. The origin of the drama has been described by Brian Arnott in an article "The Passe-Muraille Alternative":

In the summer of 1972, Paul Thompson mobilized a company of five actors and took them to the farming country near Clinton, Ontario. None save Thompson had had any measurable exposure to farming life. Each day was spent partly in visiting and working with local people and partly in a process of culling from observed reality kernels of theatrically usable material that might be refined into scenes truthfully illustrating farm life in an amusing, evocative, startling or saddening way. It was, in short, dramaturgy and performance rolled into one and practised co-operatively. It was a technique that Thompson had learned during the two years he spent with French theatrical reformer Roger Planchon in Lyons. The theatrical potential of the collective identity Planchon recognized in the French workers, Thompson saw in the Ontario farmers. The first performance of *The Farm Show* was given in the very barn where it had been developed and for the very people whose lives and identities were its subject. To this audience, every word and gesture was bursting with meaning. It was an event that contained the stuff of which great theatre is surely made.[6]

The Passe Muraille's drama went on tour in southwestern Ontario in the next year, returning to the farm community in which it had been developed, and the Ondaatje group then shot one week of the tour and filmed interviews with the actors and the director (in April 1973), returning to the Clinton area in August to film, as Ondaatje explains, "the actual characters in the play in their real settings."[7] Thus, "The Clinton Special" does not document, as it may seem to, the first period of *The Farm Show*'s progress but is retrospective when it is getting at the early difficulties of the experiment. However, those first experiences were still fresh in everyone's mind a year later, and the film does, on the whole, an admirable job of elaborating the initial confusions, frustrations and gratifications in the development of the drama. The film reveals, for example, through the Miles Potter interview, that the company was sure at the inception – when it departed Toronto for the farms of the Maitland and 16th Lines – that director Paul Thompson had a script in mind. The script, as it turned out, was evolved totally from the culture of the farm community. And the film has the perspicacity to show that at least one actor, David Fox, had doubts even after the development and success of *The Farm Show*. Fox wondered whether the production – even after the actors' live-in experiences – was not, finally, a rather superficial treatment of the community's experience. To some extent, the fiddler and tap dancers, picked up in the film, give support to Fox's view – here, in the realm of entertainment itself, is something out of reach of Passe-Muraille's sophistication. However, if there was also a political aspect to what Fox was saying, a sense perhaps that controlling divisions in the community were overlooked in the drama, the film misses it.

The problems in "The Clinton Special" seem to be ones of mood and direction. From the beginning the film builds quite skilfully toward the performance of *The Farm Show*. There are interviews with the director, the actors and various persons in the farm community, as well as shots of the rural settings and the first places of performance. A certain expectation is created, which is rewarded by the long sequence showing Miles Potter's hay-baling routine before a very appreciative local audience. Potter is an amazingly gifted and funny actor, so that when the film breaks away from him and from the rest of this particular performance of *The Farm Show*, it is doubly disappointing. At that point, the film must win us over once again. (The problem may have been technical; Ondaatje explained in the *Rune* interview that filming of *The Farm Show* itself had to be done in four nights of performance, on $500 and with such equipment as was available. "One of the cameras got broken and in the auction barn, for example, a lot of the stuff from the barn was ruined."[8])

Another problem of mood and direction is posed by the Charlie Wilson sequence near the end. In this sequence, it seems to me, the filmmaker selects the final direction in which the interpretation of the rich materials of the film should go. Ondaatje might have chosen another mood and direction for this kind of statement. Drawing upon the interview with Paul Thompson, for example, he might have chosen to emphasize the dramaturgical point: "Put people on stage, in any kind of thickness, and they are interesting to watch." He might have chosen to underscore the importance of the regional and Canadian orientation of the work. What the Charlie Wilson sequence emphasizes, however, is 'myth' and 'mythology,' following up Thompson's interview statement about theatre production in Canada, "You have to create your own mythology." Of this part of *The Farm Show*, Ondaatje has said,

The Charlie Wilson scene was one that obsessed me from the first time that I saw the play. One of the things that knocks me out every time I see that scene is where somebody is talking about Charlie's coming over every Saturday night to watch *Bonanza*, you know, totally unaware that he himself is a myth and that *Bonanza* is third rate mythology.[9]

But the impetus and richness of *The Farm Show* and the earlier part of the film is not so easily reduced to, or summed up, in a single character, no matter what the legend. The comic and celebratory spirit of *The Farm Show* is caught from a sense of community, and the film must, in a decisive way, acknowledge a debt to, and a sympathy for, the vision of community if it is to fully reflect Passe Muraille's accomplishment. To some extent, of course, community is there in the stories about Charlie Wilson, but the 'myth' has a higher profile in the telling than the common focus of activity which can give rise to such narrative.

Nevertheless, "The Clinton Special" is a strong work, offering many levels of reflection on experience, art, and community. It deserves to be one of our most familiar films.

CHAPTER SEVEN

Throes of Modernism

Sur le champ de bataille, les membres séparés
s'agitent comme autant d'animaux.
DIDEROT, *Éléments de physiologie*

CRITICAL use of the term *modernism* has often taken an unfortunate middle way, between the narrow use of the term to refer to cultural movements which so labelled themselves and the sort of usage which encompasses the *episteme* of a period. The middle way has been to load the term *modernism* with some sense of broad historical relevance and yet to make the application of the term heavily depend upon the relations among certain works of literature and of other arts. The method, in the case of Cyril Connolly's *The Modern Movement,* was to identify a period on the basis of literary works which were most accessible by the standard of contemporary experience: "1880 seems to me the point at which the Modern Movement can be diagnosed as an event which is still modern to us, more modern than many of us, not something put away in the moth-balls of history."[1] Or, in the case of the superficially more exact definition offered by Malcolm Bradbury and James McFarlane, the method was to conflate a number of declared "modernist" movements and a critical tradition holding the early decades of the century to be the heyday of modernist characteristics. An immediate difficulty with such approaches – and the number of examples could be multiplied almost indefinitely – is that, contrary to the soundest historical approach of finding the dynamic in the contradictions of a period, it becomes necessary for critics of the middle way to reject some writers of the period, to deal gingerly with others, and to be very selective as to what examples will be "typical" of the artistic features in question. Yet another writer on the subject, Irving Howe, has found it necessary to apologize for the lack of a definitive treatment, though arguing that in the nature of the case, this may be impossible anyway: "Nor will I try to provide a neatly shaped synthesis of what modernism may be, for I neither have such an idea in mind nor believe it would be useful if I did."[3] The other treatments cited above offer similar evasions; this is commonplace in the tactics of criticism. But one must wonder what value there can be in offering to discuss an abstraction which necessarily has only the most piecemeal and arbitrary historical reference and lacks the exposition appropriate to a philosophical concept. The principle difficulties in treatments of modernism which go the middle way arise from the modernist *episteme* itself. Indeed, in each of the works cited, testimonials are given to the enduring positive influence of modernism, and the impression is often created in such criticism that the writing is not merely close to its subject but engulfed by it. Some of the symptoms of the modernist bind in this criticism: 1. standing on professionalism, in terms of canon or of arguing from specialized literary or art history; 2. a progressive view of the modernist achievement; 3. psychological explanation of individuals and individual works and also of more inclusive historical phenomena.

To establish the structure of the assumptions, or the *episteme*, of an historical period, it's necessary not only to examine the real and imagined departures from the *episteme,* the decay of the synthesis, but also to locate the apogee of the period, in which the synthesis had its most pervasive hegemony, and to indicate a background to this time, during which the assumptions took shape and were increasingly well-integrated as a platform for thought. The difficulty with labelling a certain literary or artistic upheaval "modernism" and then proceeding to analyze it on its own terms is that it begs the question as to whether such change represents a decisive historical break or is really only a recycling of tired assumptions or pointless experiments. Avant-gardism itself is a case in point; from the recent work of art critics such as Kenneth Coutts-Smith, we can now understand more clearly its relation to hegemonic assumptions about progress which go back to the heyday of the 19th-century synthesis. The historical weight of social structures, and particularly of those formalized structures which serve political and economic forces, is, after all, not to be pushed aside by revolutions in prosody, and one essential question about a new artistic direction therefore is "In what sense is this only another translation of the received thought of the time?" Getting the answer means going back to the *episteme* of the period, attempting to see the work in an historical context which includes not only artistic influences and various individual professions of thought but also the propaganda and chatter of hegemonic social relations. Seen in this way, the artistic and ideological trends laying a claim to the new are often quite unexceptional; in literature, the differences between the experimental and the conventional are often muted, less essential for understanding than the root similarities.

Yet there's a danger in trying to get at the assumptions which gave rise, by reaction or transmutation, to all the little modernisms, to the piecemeal account of the modern in criticism. The danger comes from the fact that, no matter how elegantly particular features of the *episteme* have been overturned by individual writers, the assumptions of the 19th-century synthesis are still the legitimating ideology of governments and other hegemonic social institutions and formations in the West. Power in Western societies, of whatever political label, lives and breathes a "refuted" discourse, and its structure and survival depends on this discourse. The danger in yet another "refutation" of what I want to call the modernist *episteme* is in the illusion that critical or philosophical or historical refutations can, in themselves, bring down structures of such long history and pervasive influence – can lead, perhaps, to something we would call "postmodernism." In fact, as most of us feel, humanity will be fortunate to escape the West's impoverished formulas of legitimacy short of a global disaster.

While there are differences of opinion as to the ancestry or origin of the various parts of the modernist *episteme,* there is little critical disagreement that by the mid-19th-century, there was, in the West, an integration of world-view with pervasive influence. One can see the elements of this integration most clearly in the work of this time and of the period to the eve of the Great War; once these elements emerge in their relations, it becomes possible to trace earlier and piecemeal attempts at such an integration in the late 18th century as well as lines of disintegration and translation down to the present.

Within the limits of this chapter, it must suffice to present, as concisely as possible, a number of elements of what I've called the modernist *episteme* in an effort to provide a meaningful definition of *modernism* for the discussion of Ondaatje's work which follows.[A]

A By way of apology for offering still another definition of modernism, it should be pointed out that, so far as the historical dimensions of modernism are concerned, a number of contemporary Canadian writers have been brought within the scope of this term, and Western writers antedating the 1890 or 1880 limit have been granted

Some of the root concepts, then, of the modernist synthesis:

1. The findings of the natural and human sciences are in principle – and with regard to particular areas of knowledge, are in fact – logically unified and consistent, universally and timelessly true.

2. The development of the sciences is inherently progressive and is the guarantee of general historical progress – directly, through the control of natural forces, and indirectly, through the fostering of a truth-centred and truth-seeking ethos.

3. The workings of mind can be scientifically revealed by methods and theoretical models drawn from the natural sciences. A general psychology is possible.[4]

4. Scientific work and the scientific ethos necessary to undertake it

modernist characteristics in a wide range of critical work. Collingwood's point (in *The Idea of History*) that history is, essentially, the history of thought is relevant in considering the usage of terms such as *modernism, neoclassicism, romanticism* etc.; if the definition of such terms doesn't offer a basis for a creative dialectic, which promises, interactively, new historical understanding and further refinements of the concepts themselves, then they are obviously not of much use.

An objection might be raised, however, that there are simpler or more obvious definitions of *modernism* than the one offered in this chapter. There is no proving a negative, but perhaps it would be useful to consider one such definition of some currency – "modernism is innovation." In other words, the criterion for deciding whether a literary work is modernist is whether it represents an innovative departure from previous work. What are the problems with this? First, there's the concept of innovation itself; the characteristics of innovation in the sciences probably can't be safely applied to literary works, while the study of cultural innovation (from anthropology) offers a complex, far from ready-made, approach. Second, innovation is not only the mark of the artist's creative will, it is also a symptom of disintegrating or discordant cultural standards. As experiment expresses a failure or negation of value, the meaning of innovation itself can be undercut. Finally, what happens when we actually try to apply this criterion? Limiting ourselves to the period 1900-1930, how would we compare modernism in Dreiser and Wells with modernism in Joyce, or would this comparison be desirable? After all, there is innovative subject matter in both science fiction and naturalistic fiction. If some kinds of of innovation are excluded from consideration, in the criticism of modernism, the application of the term becomes fraught with all sorts of evaluative and logical difficulties. For example, if *stylistic* innovation becomes the principle criterion, then this kind of innovation must be characterized with serviceable accuracy; works must be evaluated in terms of this characterization and included in, or excluded from, the concept of modernism accordingly; and the works must be shown to belong, at the very least, to a coherent history of literary influences and development, largely independent of the literature they have been contrasted with. On the other hand, if the criterion of innovation is used in a broad sense (Wells cheek by jowl with Joyce), one is led on to the need for an historical understanding of the diversity of changes thus considered – something which obviates the use of a simple definition.

(disinterestedness, suspended judgment, etc.) have their source in a consciousness, a rationality, a certain order of mind etc. which can effectively overrule other motivations.

5. Aesthetic judgments, or judgments of feeling (including those related to the arts), are radically individual ('subjective' or 'personal') and lack the truth-value, either in degree or kind, of scientific judgments.[B]

6. A term or schematization of irrational experience is needed which brings it within the ambit of scientific knowledge, as subject matter, and thereby legitimates its uses.[C]

7. The scientific enterprise and all concomitant enterprises – such as progressive industrial management – are necessarily supported by specialized endeavour as sanctioned by social needs and, with still more certainty, by institutional requirements for expertise. In turn, specialization and professionalization are legitimized by the enterprises they serve and have the authority of primary knowledge (as contrasted with the uncertainties associated with aesthetic and moral judgments).[D]

8. The root justification of moral judgments, when it can be given, must be essentially scientific in character, stemming from institutions or social formations which have such authority, or, more directly, from findings in the life or human sciences (usually, in biology, economics, or psychology).[E]

9. The industrial association of workers in efficient production and consumption is inherently progressive.[F]

B This refers only to the domain of feeling within modernism. There have been, of course, forms of aestheticism which aped scientific judgments or structures.

C Though there were plenty of earlier formulations related to religious and psychological approaches (for example, Swedenborgianism, Mesmerism and animal magnetism, French materialism, somnambulism, spiritualism, *Naturphilosophie*, transcendentalism, etc.), it was Eduard von Hartmann's achievement in 1868 to locate this term – which he called *das Unbewusste* (the Unconscious) – in the context necessary to uphold its legitimacy with flexibility and continued success. While offering a term which still mediated between irrational conflicts and needs and a scientific world-view, von Hartmann situated the term by way of physiological and psychological illustration and was careful to indicate that it could be squared, as required, with the encroachments of naturalistic description: "Wherever consciousness is able to replace the Unconscious, it ought to replace it...." From: Eduard von Hartmann, *Philosophy of the Unconscious: Speculative Results According to the Inductive Method of Physical Science,* trans. William Chatterton Coupland, vol. II (New York: MacMillan & Co., 1884), p. 41.

This is not intended to be an exhaustive list of the ruling assumptions of modernism; undoubtedly, other elements of the essential *episteme* could be specified. However, it must be emphasized that the instancing of particular theoretical structures, such as Darwin's natural selection or Marx's political economy, would be quite beside the point since the function of the list is to outline a hegemonic view within which a very great proportion of the intellectual activity of the period – notwithstanding the variety of that activity – has found its orientation.

One general epistemic concern missing from the list is language, and perhaps a succinct formulation of the modernist view can be found. As many modernist writers have recognized, language is a particularly recalcitrant subject matter for scientific comprehension. On the other hand, there are identifiable trends within modernism concerned with: a) synthesizing language to create a more efficient medium for scientific thought and for international communication (and, more recently, to create a model of "thought itself"); b) grounding the orderliness of thought in an *a priori* capacity for

D Concerning this process, Alasdair MacIntyre has written: "Civil servants and managers alike justify themselves and their claims to authority, power and money by invoking their own competence as scientific managers of social change. Thus there emerges an ideology which finds its classical form of expression in a pre-existing sociological theory, Weber's theory of bureaucracy. Weber's account of bureaucracy notoriously has many flaws. But in his insistence that the rationality of adjusting means to ends in the most economical and efficient way is the central task of the bureaucrat and that therefore the appropriate mode of justification of his activity by the bureaucrat lies in the appeal to his (or later her) ability to deploy a body of scientific and above all social scientific knowledge, organized in terms of and understood as comprising a set of universal law-like generalisations, Weber provided the key to much of the modern age" (MacIntyre, p. 82).

E From French materialism to sociobiology, a good deal of effort has been expended on demonstrating the "natural" basis of valid moral judgments. That such arguments are essentially arbitrary but are, nonetheless, repeatedly advanced, and often with great impact, suggests the resilience and the influence of this particular assumption.

F As John Zerzan indicates in his article "Origins and Meaning of World War I," in the decades prior to the Great War there was a widespread consensus, embracing a range of European societies and of social formations within them, that socialism or some kindred social or economic revolution was not only desirable but historically inevitable. The success of the Bolsheviks notwithstanding, the organization of national war efforts and the war's immense destruction defused much of the prewar impetus for revolutionary change. (Zerzan's article appears in: *Telos*, No. 49, fall, 1981, pp. 97-116.)

language; and c) developing an analysis of language which permits a purified or formalized system of signs to meet the requirements of scientific systematicity and comprehensiveness. From considerations such as these, it's clear that there are characteristic modernist approaches to language but that these have not had the currency or the hegemonic influence of the elements of the *episteme* given above.

One further comment before taking up the work of Ondaatje in this context: The view of modernism which I'm advancing invites a search for refuting instances; surely, the reader will say, even in the period which I've designated the climax of modernism (roughly, from the 1830s to the years before the Great War), there must be many influential intellectuals, and many others as well, who did not stand upon the modernist criteria I've given. At the risk of some repetition, I want to give at least the outline of a reply to this objection. In the first place, the criteria of modernism do not rule out the existence of survivals from earlier periods. Rather, what is being argued is that such survivals were less influential, even less explicable on their own terms, as the modernist synthesis came together. The latter by no means silenced all views inconsistent with itself, but it did exercise a hegemonic influence, linked with the powers of institutions and social formations, on the character of discourse. Specific figures may be instanced in opposition to certain of the modernist criteria (perhaps Kierkegaard, Nietzsche, Flaubert or Ernst Mach, to give the first examples that come to mind), but the criteria must be understood and interrelated, as imposing a kind of double-bind on the intellectual activity of the times. Did the aestheticists really oppose the modernist *episteme* or did they make use of certain 'escape clauses' which were actually part of that totality?[G] Nietzsche, self-characterized in *Joyful Wisdom* (*Die fröhliche Wissenschaft*) as one who "resists the whole spirit of his age, stops it at the door and calls it to account," sustained a moral theory which, in Alasdair MacIntyre's words,

depends upon the truth of one central thesis: that all rational vindications of morality manifestly fail and that *therefore* belief in tenets of morality needs to be explained in terms of a set of rationalisations which conceal the fundamentally non-rational phenomena of the will.[5]

G Consider Oscar Wilde's "The Soul of Man under Socialism," the implicit progressivism of "the new work of art is beautiful by being what Art has never been" and a concluding thought: "It [the modern world] trusts to socialism and to science as its methods. What it aims at is an Individualism expressing itself through joy."

Does this line of thought, or any other, mean that Nietzsche had quite overcome the modernist criteria in question? MacIntyre places Nietzsche in a history of the fragmentation of the basis of moral judgments and compares his brilliant analysis of the lack of essential authority in accepted morality with the arbitrary forms of moral authority assumed by institutional figures such as managers, therapists, and bureaucrats.[6] But even MacIntyre's succinct statement of Nietzsche's thesis suggests the complementarity, the unendingly reinforced double-bind, between modernist notions of the irrational and the rational. From *Joyful Wisdom* again: "Where has logic originated in men's heads? Undoubtedly, out of the illogical, the domain of which must originally have been immense." It is being too dogmatic to argue that individual intellect never triumphs in opposition – to reject the whole spirit of the age seems somehow typical of modernism in any case. But, especially in a world which knows its own mind as the late 19th century did, the result of opposition must often be an empty form of resistance without the influence or the authority which is sought. Perhaps I should add that, in my own reading, the earliest Western writer in which I find a nearly complete rejection of modernism on other than traditionalist grounds is R.G. Collingwood.

*

Chapter 3 considered Ondaatje's striking, often violent imagery from one perspective; here I'd like to approach this topic from another point of view. The violent image may be the feature of Ondaatje's poetry which is most frequently discussed, sometimes with the implication that it is novel or exceptional. Certainly there is violence of imagery throughout his work, and a poem such as "For John, Falling" (from *The Dainty Monsters*) suggests that his skill in handling such imagery was accomplished even in the early work. In the long poem *Tin Roof,* published in 1982, there seems to be an explicit, if oblique, recognition of the translation of experience in this way:

It is impossible to enter the sea here
except in a violent way

Something which links the various instances in which Ondaatje uses this sort of imagery is what might be called its 'magical naturalism.'

That is, the imagery is generally a vivid depiction of, or extrapolation from, natural detail, and there is at least a naturalistic fatalism which emerges now and then, as in the final lines of "Pig Glass":

Comfort that bites through skin
hides in the dark afternoon of my pocket.
Snake shade.
Determined histories of glass. (*TK* 85)

One of the extended expressions of this kind is the narrative of Lalla's death in *Running in the Family,* which ends:

... Lalla fell into deeper waters, past the houses of 'Cranleigh' and 'Ferncliff.' They were homes she knew well, where she had played and argued over cards. The water here was rougher and she went under for longer and longer moments coming up with a gasp and then pulled down like bait, pulled under by something not comfortable any more, and then, there was the great blue ahead of her, like a sheaf of blue wheat, like a large eye that peered towards her, and she hit it and was dead.[7]

Especially because the imagery is fascinating in its own right, it's puzzling that its *bizarrerie* or uniqueness has been asserted or accepted at face value. The writer himself, in "King Kong Meets Wallace Stevens" from *Rat Jelly,* indicates one direction in which we might go looking for the sources of the imagery:

Meanwhile W.S. in his suit
is thinking chaos is thinking fences.
In his head – the seeds of fresh pain
his exorcising,
the bellow of locked blood. (*RJ* 61)

And one can begin to locate this writing within literary history by comparing it with, in Robert Buttel's words, "Stevens' predilection for the bizarre, the irrational, and the grotesque."[8] However, though the Stevens / Ondaatje comparison is of interest, naturalistic imagery can be seen in a longer perspective, as the sentence from Diderot at the beginning of the chapter was meant to show. Though the ostensible purpose of Diderot's *Éléments de physiologie* is to provide artists with a description of the body which would enhance the accuracy of their work, its larger purpose is to offer a consistently materialist view of physiology which, in fact, embraces all human activity. The function of certain images in the work – such as the image of severed limbs moving as so many animals – is not only to inform but also to shock, even primarily to shock, readers for whom the full implications of materialist physiology were unexplored ground. In a like manner, Zola uses naturalistic imagery for shock value almost a century later, in the climactic period of modernism, and it is not just coincidence that one of his most important statements of literary purpose, "Le Roman expérimental," derives the inspiration for its programme from a work of experimental medicine. But if Ondaatje's use of imagery has counterparts throughout modernism, there is an important respect in which it differs from the disturbing images in Diderot, in Zola, in Stevens as well: it has no programmatic intention. In fact, rather oxymoronic terms such as 'magical naturalism' and 'naturalistic fatalism' are needed to describe it because it does not rest on a coherent philosophical vision. It presents us with the effects of modernism, the strengths of style and insight which can come from natural detail, but the basis of this way of experiencing is disjointed, failed in its logic, partially replaced by something else. In this respect, and others, Ondaatje's work belongs to a larger failure of coherence, the throes of modernism.

In modernism, observation is a function of what is and is not scientific knowledge, of what may and may not belong to the systematic (natural) unity of things. Literature and its critical rationales do homage to this reality either by 1) taking in the objectives of existing sciences or 2) by distinguishing new objects which belong to a potentially scientific domain or have the truth-value of disinterested natural description or 3) by largely abandoning any pretension to primary truth. It would be a mistake, therefore, to consider the well-observed details of Ondaatje's work as something wholly arising, rather mysteriously, from an individual need to observe just those details in just that way. On the other hand, it would be a mistake to consider the apparent detachment of the writer's observations – "Not Ideas about the Thing But the Thing Itself" goes the Stevens title – untroubled by other relations to the world, including the artist's relations through the artwork itself. A quite personal allusion to such conflict emerged in "Billboards," one of the *Rat Jelly* poems:

Numerous problems I was unequal to.
Here was I trying to live
with a neutrality so great

I'd have nothing to think of,
just to sense
and kill it in the mind. (*RJ* 15)

As I've already argued, *Billy the Kid* has the same sort of tension, its observation also a mask for the conflicts – the repression and the violence – within imagination. Yet, later works hardly reveal that Ondaatje has resolved this ambivalence. The same faith in the significance of natural or objective detail and the same detachment in expressing it obtain in *Running in the Family* as obtained in *The Dainty Monsters*. It is true that he has brought his writing closer to home, and closer to the difficulties of history, over time; but an essentially modernist observation language remains, haunted, to be sure, by inexplicables and contradictions.

I want to examine Ondaatje's use of observation language in *Running in the Family*, but it may be useful to look first at a poem reacting to the scientific attitudes of a fellow poet. This is "Pure Memory / Chris Dewdney," first appearing in *The Capilano Review* in 1975. Dewdney was precocious both in poetic talent (*A Palaeozoic Geology of London, Ontario; Fovea Centralis;* etc.) and in his encyclopaedic knowledge of, and curiosity about, the natural sciences.[9] The "Pure Memory" is partly reference to the reflection on memory in *A Palaeozoic Geology* and to Dewdney's preface in that work which concludes:

A man's entire experiential memory exists only unto himself, is fractionally communicable and chronologically ephemeral.... There do exist however, certain three dimensional, universally perceptable [sic] memories posited from the workings of the evolutionary mind of form. THE FOSSIL IS PURE MEMORY.

Ondaatje's poem consists of a numbered sequence of ten reflections in prose-poem form. The self-effacement of the first section, in which he describes how he fumbled the title of Dewdney's book on a radio talk show, may seem gratuitous on first reading but already suggests an awe before the high-minded rationality of which Dewdney is an exemplar. (This seems to be the same Ondaatje who, by his own account, was forever banned from using the Coach House computers after pushing the wrong button.) In the next five sections, we get a portrait of the writer reflecting Ondaatje's first acquaintance with him. There is an obvious sympathy here with Dewdney, with his

sense of humour and his living within the science which, to most people, is uninhabitable but is, nevertheless, the acknowledged source of
first truths. Yet, there's something else in this description:

He comes to dinner, steps out of the car and transforms the 10 year old
suburban garden into ancient history. Is on his knees pointing out the age
and race and character of rocks and earth. He loves the Norfolk Pine. I give
him a piece of wood 120 million years old from the tar sands and he smokes a
bit of it. Recently he claims the rest of the piece is going white.

Dewdney is a Melquíades producing some further novelty for
Macondo. The upside down globe over the baby's crib has the
ingenuity and humour of the gypsy's demonstration of ice. We're
before the 'marvels of science.'

In the seventh segment of the poem, the mood shifts, becomes
somber, looks back to the quotation from Dewdney at the beginning
of the poem: "Listen, it was so savage and brutal and powerful that
even though it happened out of the blue I knew there was nothing
arbitrary about it." What Dewdney is describing here is his wife's
sudden suffering of a brain haemorrhage, and what Ondaatje is trying to fathom, in the poem, is Dewdney's reactions to this, the reasons, especially, of his being able to cope with this. (Of course, there
can be no wholly realized answer to this kind of inquiry, nor is it in
the nature of Ondaatje's literary approach to present an incident or a
relationship in the guise of a totality.) As Ondaatje describes
Dewdney's face in the seventh segment, there is a suggestion of the
survival of something deeper than the day-to-day actor, the man
manipulating a computer typesetting terminal, and the suggestion
has the weight of Dewdney's own sentence, "The fossil is pure
memory." Yet the earlier Dewdney persists as well, perhaps somewhat incongruously in Ondaatje's eyes:

... he has bought two mounted butterflies for a very good price. If I don't tell
anyone he will let me know where I could get one. A Chinaman in London
Ontario sells them. I start to laugh. He doesn't. This is serious information,
important rare information like the history of rocks – these frail wings of
almost powder have their genealogies too.

The imagery of these last segments of the poem suggests a
transvaluation of commonplaces – the movie "Earthquake," a
poster of James Dean, reading Frank O'Hara – in Dewdney's perspective. As with Billy, quite ordinary fields of experience unexpect-

edly offer sources of discovery and conflict. And it is with Billy that Ondaatje's characterization of Dewdney asks to be compared.

Yet, this comparison is perhaps not even implied in the poem, which offers a sympathetic, protective portrait from beginning to end. That this is the intention of the portrait becomes ironically explicit, in fact:

On the bus going back to Toronto I have a drawing of him by Bob Fones. Wrapped in brown paper it lies above me on the luggage rack. When the bus swerves I put my arm out into the dark aisle ready to catch him if it falls. (*TK* 150-103)

However, as soon as we realize that Dewdney, as characterized, may inhabit the same landscape of horrific reasons-why that Ondaatje unfolded in *Billy the Kid,* we reach an impasse: either Ondaatje has recognized this region of identity but has chosen to ignore it or he doesn't perceive that Dewdney's exemplary consciousness belongs to the same code as the repressive imagination of the earlier work. On one level, *Billy the Kid* surely does suggest the revival of a philosophical view which, in Feyerabend's words,

draws a clear distinction between a *natural knowledge* that is accessible to all and guides [people] in their relations to nature and their fellow men and the intellectual tumours, also called 'knowledge' that have assembled around it and have almost made it disappear.[10]

But it isn't a comprehensive rejection of modernist consciousness, notwithstanding its sometimes vigorous dialectic. Ondaatje hasn't pulled his punches in the Dewdney poem – the awe and admiration are genuine. With some reserve, even with humour, he accepts the homage in Dewdney's work to a higher scientific consciousness. He has by no means rejected the premises of modernism, however much his work is invaded by the expression of something alien to it.

This sense that in reading Ondaatje, we're not looking for a consistently modernist expression or for a comprehensive rejection of modernism is important in attempting to understand the conflicting epistemic premises of the writing in *Running in the Family.* What are these? In the first place, there's the premise that the family story is something to be built up from oral history,[H] from the spoken words of those who know something of the Ondaatje family's past.

H In the discussion which follows, *history* is often used in a broad sense or conventionally.

Ondaatje is aware that this is a somewhat uncertain process. For personal reasons, recollection will be very selective in character:

Truth disappears with history and gossip tells us in the end nothing of personal relationships. There are stories of elopements, unrequited love, family feuds, and exhausting vendettas, which everyone was drawn into, had to be involved with. But nothing is said of the closeness between two people.... [11]

As well, there is the 'public' reticence of the inquirer. Moreover, recollected incident must be given some finality and authenticity of form, in some instances must pass through many stages of meaning before reaching a final version:

In the heart of this 250-year-old fort we will trade anecdotes and faint memories, trying to swell them with the order of dates and asides, interlocking them all as if assembling the hull of a ship. No story is ever told just once. Whether a memory or funny hideous scandal, we will return to it an hour later and retell the story with additions and this time a few judgements thrown in. In this way history is organized. [12]

But, although comments and exchanges from this process – carefully recorded – are presented here and there in the book with the authority of fact, *Running in the Family* is not only premised upon this kind of narrative.

The oral history is actually bracketed by Ondaatje's characteristic observation language, a distanced and precise description of, in the main, 'objective' features of natural phenomena and social incident. Much of this description is given in a journal-like accounting, but this shift in style is not important for the basic premise, its essence a language in a broadly naturalistic literary tradition.

However, these epistemic bases are not sufficient for what Ondaatje wants to accomplish, and there is a further premise of this kind in the writing. There is what I've called the 'magical naturalism' of Lalla's death (in "The Passions of Lalla" section); this sort of writing appears also in the most directly fictional attempt to describe his father, "'Thanikama,'" and is interjected elsewhere in the book, as in Ondaatje's imagery of a "human pyramid" in "Jaffna Afternoons." What these passages have in common is their imaginary experience, their evasion of the immediacy of recorded conversation, present events, and present environment. Of course, the writing still wears the guise of such immediacy, but the structure of the narrative – even more so than recollection of the past, which can always be encapsulated in the present – requires the recognition of a validity of narrative which doesn't fully belong to the real. Ondaatje's own understanding of this is tersely produced in the acknowledgements at the end of the book; referring to a long list of "relatives, friends and colleagues who helped me in my inquisitiveness," Ondaatje adds:

While all these names may give an air of authenticity, I must confess that the book is not a history but a portrait or 'gesture.' And if those listed above disapprove of the fictional air I apologize and can only say that in Sri Lanka a well-told lie is worth a thousand facts.[13]

This can scarcely be an apology in advance for factual errors or mistakes in judgment, much less an admission of indifference as to the truth-value of the work. What Ondaatje does seem to be saying is that, even if narrative deceives, offers entertaining illusions in contrast with the straight medicine of reality, there is a kind of narrative which can transcend this limitation – "a well-told lie is worth a thousand facts." This line of thought suggests Ondaatje's early interest in myth and archetype, and it may be that this is what he had in mind in writing the above passage though if this sort of consideration is present in *Running in the Family,* its influence is more *ad hoc* than systematic. Interestingly, the book's direct accounts of Sri Lankan custom such as "Tongue" or the poem "High Flowers" are more folkloric than archetypal in feel.

So here are at least three different modes in which the truth-value of Ondaatje's narrative is premised: 1) oral history, 2) observation language, and 3) imaginary experience. The book reconciles these premises and, at one level, there is perhaps nothing very surprising about that. But, since the value attached to each method derives from modernism, their presentation side by side, with little mediating assurance as to their connections, poses a question about the basis of coherence in the work. However, the point bears repeating that the lack of a coherent ground is not an idiosyncracy of this book or of Ondaatje's work generally but is symptomatic of what has become of the modernist *episteme.* Comparing his handling of oral history and imaginary experience with his use of an observation language reveals much about what has and hasn't been taken from modernism.

Before this comparison can be undertaken, the notion that Ondaatje's choice of literary stance involves an observation language deriving from the modernist *episteme* needs some clarification. For descriptions of observation languages used in the sciences may be very complex, and, as well, what a writer chooses to write about in the particularity of the literary work would not necessarily belong to the subject matter of any scientific discipline. What needs underscoring here is that, out of a concern to avoid a bracketed aesthetic or moral project and to attach literature to a progressive, scientific view, generations of modernist writers have experimented with a variety of observation languages, often attempting to parallel or to reflect developments in the sciences. Thus, it's not surprising that Ondaatje's writing reflects certain features of modernist scientific ideology even though it contains little specific examination of this. The photographic icons of the objectivity Ondaatje wanted to achieve in *Billy the Kid* are also there in *Running in the Family*, and there is the same puzzling equivalence, which Perry Nodelman notes, between poems, sections of prose, and interspersed photographs. Nodelman's argument about the writer's stance in the earlier work is suggestive of the problems of observation language in the later one:

The "photographer" keeps his emotional distance from the violent events he is describing, and paradoxically, his dispassionate objectivity is so disproportionate that it amounts to misrepresentation. In fact, it is the unemotional tone of *The Collected Works* that allows Ondaatje to replace the traditional legend of Billy the Kid with his own interpretation of him. The legendary outsider whose exuberance could not be restrained by the petty restrictions of a narrowminded society was at least passionately involved in the act of living; Ondaatje's Billy is as objective about himself as a photographer is about his subjects.[14]

The point to be taken from this here is, this objectivity does not simply belong to Billy's character, it is the stance of Ondaatje's own literary language. Sometimes this language betrays its faith in the sufficiency of accurate description, as in the short poem "The Agatha Christie Books by the Window" in the "Pig Glass" section of *Knife*; it ends,

Nameless morning
solution of grain and colour

There is this amazing light,
colourless, which falls on the warm
stretching brain of the bulb
that is dreaming avocado (*TK* 72)

In this context, the word *dreaming* is already bracketed – literary licence which the reader will understand. More successful because exotic, the catalogue of experiences in the prose of "Monsoon Notebook (i)" has the same implication of naturalistic faith in the meaning of the observed.

The problem with the oral history, by contrast with Ondaatje's observation language, is that it necessarily has a different tone and emphasis. Ondaatje's desire for immediacy of observation leads him to give almost as much weight to the fact of recollection as to its result. This does lead to some reflection on the making of history – as already indicated – but *Running in the Family* does not take this very far. And other senses of history intervene. There is the journalistic history of "Honeymoon":

The Nuwara Eliya Tennis Championships had ended and there were monsoons in Colombo. The headlines in the local papers said, 'Lindberg's Baby Found – A Corpse!' Fred Astaire's sister, Adele, got married and the 13th President of the French Republic was shot to death by a Russian.[15]

And so on. There is the anecdotal history of the recent past – of the attempted coup of 1971.[16] And there is the scissors-and-paste history from publications, church records, gravestones, and other artifacts pertaining to the family itself. Unlike the recorded recollections of others, it is relatively simple to translate these histories into immediacy, the observation language of discovery: "When I finish there will be that eerie moment when I wash my hands and see very clearly the deep grey colour of old paper dust going down the drain."[17] Where a naturalistic mode of observation is characteristic, the intransigence of oral history derives from its attempts to recapture what was thought in the past. In at least inchoate form, oral history represents the essential matter of history as Collingwood saw it:

Historical knowledge is the knowledge of what mind has done in the past, and at the same time it is the redoing of this, the perpetuation of past acts in the present. Its object is therefore not a mere object, something outside the mind which knows it; it is an activity of thought, which can be known only in so far as the knowing mind re-enacts it and knows itself as so doing. To the historian, the activities whose history he is studying are not spectacles to be watched, but experiences to be lived through in his own mind; they are objective, or known to him, only because they are also subjective, or activities of his own.[18]

There is perhaps only one section of *Running in the Family* in which this sense of history emerges – " 'Thanikama,' " in which Ondaatje attempts directly to enter his father's experience in his last years. I want to return to this in the comments below. By contrast, Ondaatje's use of oral history documents but does not capture the intersubjectivity of the past. We are presented with a wonderful series of anecdotes, with a chain of incident, and even with some social and political reference points, but important questions are left unanswered: Was the break-up of inherited wealth only something which affected the Ondaatjes and the Gratiaens, or were there deeper social reasons for the generation of "flaming youth" which Ondaatje describes? What was the relation of the social group he characterizes to the colonial administration and to other groups and classes in Ceylon? If this social group stood outside the many political currents in its time (as Ondaatje seems to suggest), why did it do so? What was the work of managing a tea plantation or a hotel actually like? Were there no religious or cultural conflicts in these decades worth speaking of? In the oral history, each observer is made to enter a perspective as personal and sharply focused as Ondaatje's own. (This bears some resemblance to the usual style of television or film documentaries; the manipulation of others' voices may be even less obvious in print.) The observers may be observed, in turn, by way of sharply drawn vignettes, as Phyllis (an aunt) is in "Jaffna Afternoons" and as Dolly (another aunt) is in the segment "Aunts." But more often what is taken from recollection is not used to illumine the past characters of those who offer it, and, in passages here and there throughout the book and in the segments "Lunch Conversation" and "Final Days / Father Tongue," the persons recounting the past recede into anonymity. Obviously, the oral history which Ondaatje recorded is the sine qua non of the book, the narrative motor, even in edited or translated versions. Yet, it must be contained within or interpreted through his literary observation language, the hypostatizing of the present. Such a stance, inimical to the development of historical knowledge as described by Collingwood, is the product of modernist assumptions, though not necessarily of a philosophical position which Ondaatje is taking. It reflects the scientific revolt against tradition and received knowledge, and it reflects the emphasis of a dogmatic progressivism, which devalued both the meaning and the truth-value of what could be known of the past while caught up in the importance of an expanding scientific knowledge here and now. But in spite of the importance of this side of modernism to Ondaatje's practice as a writer, there is an obvious paradox in the bracketing of oral history in *Running in the Family*: The criteria of a modernist observation language, its truth inherent in its formal objectivity, dictate that oral history, with its diversity and uncertainties, be shaped to its demands while the validity of the story which Ondaatje sought depends upon accounts which are, in some sense, falsified by literary manipulation.

The escape from this paradox is provided by modernism, and it lies in a schematization of irrational experience which brings it within the ambit of Ondaatje's literary objectivity. Thus, what I've called the "imaginary experiences" in the book are not a flight from the naturalistic real but have a near relationship to it. The mystification of the unknown is complementary to modernist consciousness and finds expression in a good deal of his work. "White Dwarfs" (from *Rat Jelly*) is an interesting example from the shorter poems; it skilfully suggests, from various bearings, occult extremes of sensibility ("Why do I love most / among my heroes those / who sail to that perfect edge / where there is no social fuel") and concludes:

This white can grow
is fridge, bed,
is an egg – most beautiful
when unbroken, where
what we cannot see is growing
in all the colours we cannot see

there are those burned out stars
who implode into silence
after parading in the sky
after such choreography what would they wish to speak of
anyway (*RJ* 71)

Two things to note about this: Its appeal to the unknown for its own sake, and the effective handling of concrete detail so that we believe a more than elusive significance is being realized in the poem. The credo of archetypal imagery has provided, in the best modernist style, a field for situating the unknown, and this has been influential in contemporary Canadian writing and is undoubtedly an influence in Ondaatje's work, though not necessarily as a systematic point of view. A number of remarks he has made about dream and myth, two sources of corroboration for archetypalism, support this conclusion. There may be, as well, in archetypalism certain natural signs of the transcendent objectivity of the irrational, as always in modernism, qualified by a hegemonic rationality. A good example of this last characteristic is the poem "Uswetakeiyawa," which appeared with the sections of *Running in the Family* published in *The Capilano Review* in 1979 and also appeared in *Knife* but was not included in *Running in the Family*. The landscape of the poem is a waking dream of night travel "returning from Colombo"; it is "unphotographed country," something which Ondaatje recognizes could not be captured in such exact imagery, and one of the natural signs of its transcendence is the dogs

who lean out of night
strolling the road
with eyes of sapphire
and hideous body
        so mongrelled
they seem to have woken
to find themselves tricked
into outrageous transformations

As in this night, Ondaatje must rely on "the imagination's / story behind each smell," he, nevertheless, does not eschew the thingness of natural detail or offer a speculative conclusion which puts aside the rational order he assumes:

... something we have never been able to recognize.
There is just this thick air
and the aura of dogs
in trickster skin.

Once in the night we saw
something slip into the canal.
There was then the odour we did not recognize.
The smell of a dog losing its shape.

But the end of the poem does point us in the direction of transcendence.

Dreams and dream-like states, myths, natural signs, and also fictive narration are all imaginary experiences within modernism, yet may all belong to the field of the irrational which modernism accepts as the complement of actual and potential scientific knowledge. Not surprisingly, for modernism's irrational to appear in the guise of knowledge, it must assume the cloak of its opposite, as a certain manner of observation, documentation and argument. Whatever the specific theoretical background of Ondaatje's use of imaginary experiences, they stand in this fundamental modernist relationship to the reality he wishes to describe. When the first pages of *Running in the Family* mention "nightmare" and "the bright bone of a dream," we have the cues that the ineffable is being touched upon, that the communications to follow do not belong to the common order of reality.

Another segment, also early in the book, complicates the relationship between the imagery and the real perhaps just because Ondaatje was not satisfied with the dream device:

That night, I will have not so much a dream as an image that repeats itself. I see my own straining body which stands shaped like a star and realize gradually I am part of a human pyramid. Below me are other bodies that I am standing on and above me are several more, though I am quite near the top. With cumbersome slowness we are walking from one end of the huge living room to the other.[19]

The contrived feel of this comes from its being neither fish nor fowl. It is not recorded as a suitably categorized imaginary experience because the writer has explicitly rejected that possibility; on the other hand, the language still leads us on in a quest after mysteries ("I see my own straining body ... and realize gradually") though how such narrative can be valid, in modernist terms, is nowhere apparent. However, this is not to say that Ondaatje's narrative line here escapes modernist concerns; after all, that troublesome explanation was still necessary: "That night, I will have not so much a dream as an image that repeats itself." Someone less concerned about the difference between the observed and the imaginary might have begun "That night, I see my own straining body" etc.

The complication of this paragraph about a human pyramid occurs again in the much more significant prose section titled "The Passions of Lalla." The first 14 pages of this 17-page segment follow the pattern of the observation which has gone before. The narrative is carefully constructed, in Ondaatje's distanced observation language, largely from facts garnered from oral history and from precise, naturalistic description of people and things. The early assertion that Lalla was "magical" and the foreshadowing in the first two sentences of the piece are not sufficient to suggest that the realm of plausibility extends beyond this framework. Ondaatje means to bring us into a fictive narrative with the sentence "But now she slept till noon, and in the early evening rode up to Moon Plains, her arms spread out like a crucifix behind"; for what could be the origin of this kind of detail except the intention to create a fiction? The "*Moon Plains*" heading which immediately follows this sentence also indicates some break in structure and, with its suggestion of the moon as natural sign related to the unconscious (as in Tarot), subtly cues us to the imaginary experience to follow. Ondaatje must still demarcate between the real and imaginary but attempts to do so in unobtrusive fashion. The problem with this is that narrative plausibility and continuity don't depend upon modernist canons of the real. Their source is the intersubjectivity of language as gesture, within the unities of imaginative process. Never being satisfied that Ondaatje is only extending the boundaries of the real or that, in spite of the fictive stance, some sort of transcendence is unfolding in these last pages of the segment, we must look for other points of reference. Perhaps we are both taken into the narrative by the remarkable use of detail and put off by its indulgence.

Still more direct in its handling of imaginary experience is " 'Thanikama,' " a fictive account of the loneliness and isolation of his father's last years. There are no ambiguous tags preceding the narrative in this section, and, so late in the book, it is the sort of attempt to enter Mervyn's thought which might be expected of Ondaatje's need to understand the past:

He drove along Galle Face Green where the Japanese had eventually attacked, by plane, and disappeared into the Fort whose streets were dark and quiet and empty. He loved the Fort at this hour, these Colombo nights, the windows of his car open and the breeze for the first time almost cool, no longer tepid, hitting his face with all the night smells, the perfume of closed boutiques. An animal crossed the road and he braked to a halt and watched it, strolling at its own speed for it was midnight and if a car would actually stop it could be trusted. This animal paused when it reached the pavement and looked back at the man in the white car – who still had not moved on. They gazed at each other and then the creature ran up the steps of the white building and into the post office which stayed open all night.[20]

Marvelous as this writing is, it's not really independent of the modernist assumptions which have shaped the book's perspective. Actually, the labelling of the imaginary experience of "'Thanikama'" occurs in two short prose sections preceding it. In the first of these, "Blind Faith," Ondaatje speaks directly to the issue of achieving a fictive vision of his father by comparing this with Edgar's prevention of Gloucester's suicide in *King Lear*: "Who if I look deeper into the metaphor, torments his father over an imaginary cliff."[21] The next section, "Bone," returns to the dream at the beginning of the book, presenting it this time as "a story" of archetypal or mythic dimensions; at this level, he broaches an interpretation of his father – "He had captured all the evil in the regions he had passed through and was holding it"[22] – and foreshadows the extended interpretation of "'Thanikama.'" The latter, therefore, does not represent a departure from the epistemic canons of modernism.

Another modernist premise reflected in "'Thanikama'" is its generally psychological character. This is not to overlook that here and throughout his work, Ondaatje avoids incorporating psychological jargon. But much of the writing in this section, as in significant portions of earlier work such as *Billy the Kid* and *Coming Through Slaughter*, pursues the naturalistic description of an individual, even an isolated, mind. The importance of psychology within modernism lies 1) in the naturalizing of moral qualities and the substantializing of individual character and 2) in its claims – in association with institutions – to predict the products of human action. Ondaatje's work is not apparently based on these considerations in any systematic way; but it does often assume that individuals can reveal their truth in isolation from the social, and they are viewed not through a social characterization of their thought but through incisively observed behavioural detail. The poem *Tin Roof* gives some insight into the importance of this perspective for Ondaatje:

All our narratives of sleep
a mind rumble to those inland

There is an inner, "unphotographed" landscape which he tries to discover, the matter under observation changing but the quest inward remaining "that perfect edge / where there is no social fuel." But the writer of *Tin Roof* is also aware of illusion and disillusion in this psychologizing. Of Rilke's *Duino Elegies* he says:

I have circled your book for years
like a wave combing
the green hair of the sea
kept it with me, your name
a password in the alley.
I always wanted poetry to be that
but this solitude brings no wisdom
just two day old food in the fridge,
certain habits you would not approve of.

And he concludes:

I wanted poetry to be walnuts
in their green cases
but now it is the sea
and we let it drown us,
and we fly to it released
by giant catapults
of pain loneliness deceit and vanity

*

The purpose of the foregoing analysis is not to demonstrate that the writer uses dated techniques or is a less urgent read than the latest thing in literature. Examining the modernist premises of the writing in *Running in the Family* reveals the degree of difficulty in stylistic problem-solving, a remarkable sensitivity of vision in spite of the entropic pull of modernism, and the utter economy of the work (and the utter nonsense of some reviewers who believed that the book is part travel guide). The critique of modernism leads to modernist conclusions when the essential point of the argument is that style or technical resource or choice of subject matter has been surpassed by some other prodigy in the forward march of the arts. If some other perspective does fully succeed modernism, hopefully it won't sustain the absurd notions of usable history typical of modernism – in literary practice, the notion, for example, that the usable past begins with Whitman, Baudelaire, Proust, Joyce, Williams, Olson, or somebody else. In that quite different, and quite hypothetical, climate of opinion, surely we will see that modernists, also, have important things to say?

Conclusion. Still in mid-career, Michael Ondaatje's course as an artist is undoubtedly open to as many possibilities as it has already traversed. If there is any validity to the arguments in Chapters 3 and 4, one of the key determinants of what course is to be taken will surely be his changing understanding of literary imagination. The film image and the poetic image are two different creatures, with distinct powers and limitations. The words through which he struggled to an essential view of the strife in imagination are not available to film; the apparent richness and exactness of the undefined visual are not available to the poem or the novel. Perhaps the troublesome concept of myth can shed some light on the dilemma, the 'myth' of "The Clinton Special" and of Mervyn and Lalla being, after all, different from the 'myth' of "Troy town" and of *The Man with Seven Toes*. Perhaps the shift toward history in *Coming Through Slaughter* and *Running in the Family* or toward a more complex immediacy in poems such as "Burning Hills," "Light," and *Tin Roof* indicates the direction Ondaatje will go. In any case, the difficult choices are still there, still insistent – a sure sign of vitality and promise in the artist's work.

Notes

For the sake of simplicity, no references are given in the notes to *The Dainty Monsters, The Man with Seven Toes, Rat Jelly, The Collected Works of Billy the Kid,* or *There's a Trick with a Knife I'm Learning to Do: Poems 1963-78.* Parenthetical notes in the text abbreviate these titles *DM, MWST, RJ, BK,* and *TK* respectively.

Notes to the Introduction

1 For the biographical, publishing and production information in the "Introduction," I have relied upon credits and blurbs in Ondaatje's published work, the *Manna* and *Rune* interviews cited in the bibliography, and Mark Witten's *Books in Canada* article, also cited there. The worst source of information I have come across is Ralph Gustafson's write-up in *Contemporary Poets* – a minefield.

2 Untitled interview, *Manna,* No. 1, March 1972, p. 19.

3 Sam Solecki, "An Interview with Michael Ondaatje," *Rune,* No. 2, Spring 1975, p. 48.

4 *Manna,* p. 21.

5 Ibid., p. 20.

6 *Rune,* p. 47.

7 Ibid.

8 Ibid., p. 46.

8 *Manna,* p. 20.

10 *Rune,* pp. 51-52.

11 Mark Witten, "Billy, Buddy, and Michael," *Books in Canada,* VI (June-July 1977), 12.

12 *Rune,* pp. 47-48.

13 Ibid., p. 53.

14 Ibid., p. 49.

15 Robin Skelton, "The Element of Fire Is Not Quite Put Out," *Books in Canada,* VI (November 1977), 35.

16 "*Ethos:* Selected Bibliography," *Ethos,* I (Summer 1983), 64.

17 Jon Pearce, ed., *Twelve Voices: Interviews with Canadian Poets* (Ottawa: Borealis Press, 1980), p. 133.

18 Ibid., p. 132.

19 The poems with changes in language are "Birds for Janet – The Heron," "Billboards," and "The Vault." Changes in punctuation and typography occur in "Signature" and

"Charles Darwin Pays a Visit, December 1971." Eight of the selected poems had changes in page break from the earlier books.

20 Michael Ondaatje, ed., *The Long Poem Anthology* (Toronto: The Coach House Press, 1979), p. 11.

21 For interesting comment on this and earlier productions of *Billy the Kid,* see: Max Wyman, "Billy the Kid, Baby-Faced Billy, Where Did You Go Plumb Wrong?" *The Vancouver Sun,* March 3, 1977, p. 31.

22 Cf. Benny Green, "All That Jazz," *The Spectator,* CCXLIII (September 8, 1979), 25; also, David Lancashire, "Play about Jazzman Takes Dramatic Licence," *The Globe and Mail,* CXXXVI (January 2, 1980), 13. The historical study of Bolden apparently referred to by both Lancashire and Ondaatje (in the text quotation) is: Donald M. Marquis, *In Search of Buddy Bolden: First Man of Jazz* (Baton Rouge, La.: Louisiana State University Press, 1978).

23 Pearce, p. 134.

24 John Oughton, "Sane Assassin," *Books in Canada,* XII (June / July 1983), 10.

25 Pearce, p. 140.

26 T.H. Adamowski, "The Disenchantment of the Word," *Queen's Quarterly,* LXXXVIII (Autumn 1981), 456.

27 Frank Kermode, "Institutional Control of Interpretation," *Salmagundi,* No. 43, Winter 1979, p. 86.

28 Alasdair MacIntyre, *After Virtue: A Study in Moral Theory* (Notre Dame, Ind.: University of Notre Dame Press, 1981), p. 6.

29 R.G.F. Collingwood, *The Principles of Art* (Oxford: Oxford University Press, 1958 [1938]), p. 243.

30 R.D. Laing, *The Politics of Experience and The Bird of Paradise* (Harmondsworth: Penguin Books Ltd., 1967), p. 25.

CHAPTER ONE: The Problem of Amusement Art

1 "Little Old Man," *The Fiddlehead,* No. 69, Summer 1966, p. 48; "The Dog Who Loved Bach," *Alphabet,* No. 16, September 1969, p. 92; "Pictures from the War," *Queen's Quarterly,* LXXV (Winter 1966), 540.

2 Tibor Scitovsky, *The Joyless Economy: An Inquiry into Human Satisfaction and Consumer Dissatisfaction* (Oxford: Oxford University Press, 1976), p. 54.

3 Some experimental documentation of the differences in brain wave activity between watching television and reading is cited in: Jerry Mander, *Four Arguments for the Elimination of Television* (New York: William Morrow and Company, Inc., 1978), pp. 205-211.

4 Scitovsky, pp. 76-77.

5 Collingwood, p. 78.

6 Ibid., p. 79.

7 Ibid., p. 81.

8 *Rune,* pp. 45-46.

9 Michael Ondaatje, *Coming Through Slaughter* (Toronto: House of Anansi Press, 1976), p. 95. In parenthetical notes abbreviated CS.

10 Ibid., p. 93.

11 *Rune,* p. 49.

12 Ibid., p. 46.

CHAPTER TWO: Logical Interrogation

1 Raymond Williams, *Marxism and Literature* (Oxford: Oxford University Press, 1977), p. 98.

2 Paul Feyerabend, *Against Method: Outline of an Anarchistic Theory of Knowledge* (London: NLB, 1975), pp. 273-274.

3 Friedrich Schiller, *Aesthetical and Philosophical Essays* (New York: Clark, Given & Hooper, n.d.), pp. 244-245. The volume is a reprint of the Bohn Library translation. Unfortunately, no current translation of Schiller's writings on art contains as much material. For the cited passage, cf.: Helmut Koopman and Benno von Weise, eds., "Über die Nothwendigen Grenzen beim Gebrauch Schöner Formen" 1795, *Schillers Werke*, Nationalausgabe, ed. Lieselotte Blumenthal and Benno von Weise, XXI (Weimar: Hermann Böhlaus Nachfolger, 1963), 17-18. Hereafter this work will be cited as "Über die Nothwendigen Grenzen" and the edition of Schiller's works as "Nationalausgabe."

4 As if to underscore the irrelevance to Ondaatje's book of historical details, the MacInnes account itself is not very dependable history. Cf. Michael Alexander's *Mrs. Fraser on the Fatal Shore* (New York: Simon and Schuster, 1971).

5 Schiller, *Essays*, pp. 35-36. Cf.: "Über die Äesthetische Erziehung des Menschen in Einer Reihe von Briefen" [1795], Nationalausgabe, XX (Weimar: Hermann Böhlaus Nachfolger, 1962), 311. Hereafter cited as "Über die Äesthetische Erziehung."

CHAPTER THREE: The Role of Imagination

1 Frances A. Yates, *The Art of Memory* (Chicago: The University of Chicago Press, 1966), p. 6.

2 Alan Richardson, *Mental Imagery* (London: Routledge & Kegan Paul, 1969), pp. 35-36.

3 Yates, p. 8.

4 Ibid., pp. 17-18.

5 Ibid., p. 9.

6 Joe Park Poe, *Heroism and Divine Justice in Sophocles' Philoctetes* (Leiden, Netherlands: —— 1974), p. 49.

7 Yates, p. 229.

8 Ibid., p. 251.

9 Ibid., p. 257.

10 Ibid.

11 Russell Fraser, *The War Against Poetry* (Princeton: Princeton University Press, 1970), p. 9.

12 Collingwood, p. 187.

13 Notwithstanding the importance of Kant's treatment of the imagination, the most useful Enlightenment account for the purposes of the present discussion may be Adam Smith's in *The Theory of Moral Sentiments*. Smith's reflection embraces a great diversity of private and public situations and includes perceptive comment on the arts. It also has the tactical advantage, where rethinking present-day assumptions is concerned, of holding to certain positions which antedated the modernist synthesis I describe in Chapter 7. An excellent survey of Enlightenment and Romantic writing on imagination (with, however, an unfortunate bias in favour of the latter) is available in: James Engell, *The Creative Imagination: Enlightenment to Romanticism*

(Cambridge, Mass.: Harvard University Press, 1981).

14 Schiller, *Essays*, p. 97. Cf.: "Über die Äesthetische Erziehung," pp. 379-380.
15 Ibid., p. 35. Cf.: "Über die Äesthetische Erziehung," p. 311.
16 Ibid., p. 79. Cf.: "Über die Äesthetische Erziehung," p. 359.
17 Ibid., p. 123. Cf.: "Über die Äesthetische Erziehung," p. 410.
18 Ibid., p. 248. Cf.: "Über die Nothwendigen Grenzen," p. 22.
19 Ibid., p. 240. Cf.: "Über die Nothwendigen Grenzen," p. 13.
20 Ibid., p. 233. Cf.: "Über die Nothwendigen Grenzen," p. 6.

CHAPTER FOUR: The Imaginative Process

1 Leslie Mundwiler, "Narrative Writing for Children," *The Organ*, 1 (Fall 1976), 40.
2 *The Reason Why: A Careful Collection of Many Hundreds of Reasons for Things Which, Though Generally Believed, Are Imperfectly Understood: General Science* (London: Houlston and Wright, 1864), p. 215.
3 Stephen Toulmin, *Human Understanding* (Princeton: Princeton University Press, 1972), p. 13.
4 Ibid., p. 6.
5 Ibid., p. 7.
6 Ibid., p. 127.
7 Arthur Schopenhauer, *The World as Will and Idea,* trans. R.B. Haldane and J. Kemp (Garden City, New York: Doubleday & Company, Inc., 1961 [1818]), p. 61.
8 Mary Hesse, "Models and Matter," in: *Quanta and Reality: A Symposium* (London: Hutchinson, 1962), pp. 56-57.
9 Edmund Husserl, *Cartesian Meditations: An Introduction to Phenomenology*, trans. Dorion Cairns (The Hague: Martinus Nikjhoff, 1969 [1931]), p. 102.
10 Martin Heidegger, *Poetry, Language, Thought*, trans. Albert Hofstadter (New York: Harper & Row, 1971), p. 198.
11 Ibid., p. 140.
12 Ibid., p. 120.
13 Martin Heidegger, *Kant and the Problem of Metaphysics*, trans. James S. Churchill (Bloomington: Indiana University Press, 1962 [1929]), p. 201.
14 Jean-Paul Sartre, *The Psychology of Imagination*, trans. Bernard Frechtman (New York: Washington Square Press, Inc., 1966 [1940]), p. 159.
15 For a categorization of experienced imagery, see: Mike Samuels and Nancy Samuels, *Seeing with the Mind's Eye: The History, Techniques and Uses of Visualization* (New York: Random House Inc., 1975), pp. 39-55.
16 Sartre, p. 78.
17 Ibid., pp. 151-152.
18 Ibid.
19 Collingwood, p. 246.
20 Ibid., p. 219.
21 Ibid., p. 194.
22 Ibid., p. 222.
23 Ibid., p. 223.
24 As a corrective to this account, the reader should consult Mary Warnock's excellent discussion *Imagination* (Berkeley, Calif.: University of California Press, 1978). Warnock's thought about the phenomenologists' handling of the subject is

informative in basis and original in scope and implications. She concludes: "For my part I have no doubt that what we may call the phenomenological tradition, and this includes Ryle, offers a better way of describing mental images than the empiricist, or Humean, tradition before it, but has not, even so, got it completely right." (P. 156.) Elsewhere she remarks: "... paradoxically, although phenomenologists exclude imagination from our perceptive awareness of the world, yet the role of imagination in this awareness becomes clearer the more one considers the theory which attempts to do without it." (P. 144.)

25 Maurice Merleau-Ponty, *The Primacy of Perception and Other Essays,* ed. James M. Edie (Evanston, Illinois: Northwestern University Press, 1964), p. 70.

26 Ibid., p. 71.

27 Ibid., p. 44.

28 Maurice Merleau-Ponty, *Phenomenology of Perception,* trans. Colin Smith (London: Routledge & Kegan Paul, 1962 [1945]), p. 385.

29 Ibid., p. 179.

30 Ibid., p. 184.

31 Ibid., p. 186.

32 Maurice Merleau-Ponty, *Adventures of the Dialectic,* trans. Joseph Bien (Evanston, Illinois: Northwestern University Press, 1973 [1955]), p. 156.

33 Ibid., pp. 137-138.

34 Ibid., p. 157.

35 Ibid., p. 138n.

36 Ibid., p. 204.

37 Maurice Merleau-Ponty, *The Visible and the Invisible,* trans. Alphonso Lingis and ed. Claude Lefort (Evanston, Illinois: Northwestern University Press, 1968), p. 92.

38 Ibid.

39 Ibid., pp. 238-239.

40 Ibid.

41 Ibid., p. 244.

42 Ibid., p. 262.

43 Ibid., pp. 264-265.

44 Ibid., p. 149.

45 There is some interesting corroboration of this in the recent finding that in the Twandan culture, formalized 'mythical' structures take up material from a diversity of oral narratives. Luc de Heuch, "Mythologie et littérature," *L'Homme,* XVII (Avril-Septembre 1977), 101-109.

46 *Rune,* p. 46.

47 Ibid., p. 47.

48 Michael Ondaatje, "Outlaws, Light and Avocadoes: Poems," *The Canadian Forum,* LIV (March 1975), p. 25.

49 Dennis Lee, *Savage Fields: An Essay in Literature and Cosmology* (Toronto: House of Anansi Press, 1977), p. 44.

50 Ibid., pp. 43-44.

51 Leslie Mundwiler, "Heidegger and Poetry," *Open Letter,* 2nd series, No. 3, Fall 1972, pp. 56-57.

52 Lee, p. 111.

53 Richardson, pp. 36-37.

CHAPTER FIVE: Tragic Bathos

1 Michael Ondaatje, *Leonard Cohen* (Toronto: McClelland and Stewart Ltd., 1970), pp. 43-44.
2 Leroi Jones [Amiri Baraka], *Black Music* (New York: William Morrow and Co., Inc., 1967), p. 15.
3 Margaret Atwood, *Survival: A Thematic Guide to Canadian Literature* (Toronto: House of Anansi Press, 1972), p. 37.
4 Schiller, *Essays*, pp. 153-154. Cf.: "Über die Pathetische" [1793], Nationalausgabe, xx (Weimar: Hermann Böhlaus Nachfolger, 1962), 200. Hereafter "Über die Pathetische."
5 Schiller, *Essays*, p. 149. Cf.: "Über die Pathetische," p. 196.
6 Ibid., p. 67. Cf.: "Über die Äesthetische Erziehung," pp. 343-344.
7 R.D. Laing, *The Divided Self: An Existential Study in Sanity and Madness* (Baltimore: Penguin Books, 1965), p. 89.

CHAPTER SIX: The Films

1 *Rune,* p. 40.
2 Raymond Williams, *The Country and the City* (St. Albans: Paladin, 1975), p. 295.
3 *Rune,* p. 40.
4 Lea Hindley-Smith et al., "Therafields," *The Canadian Forum,* LII (January 1973), p. 16.
5 *Rune,* p. 42.
6 Brian Arnott, "The Passe-Muraille Alternative," in *The Human Elements,* ed. David Helwig (Oberon Press, 1978), p. 104.
7 *Rune,* p. 45.
8 Ibid.
9 Ibid., p. 44.

CHAPTER SEVEN: Throes of Modernism

1 Cyril Connolly, *The Modern Movement: One Hundred Key Books from England, France and America, 1880-1950* (London: Andre Deutsch / Hamish Hamilton, 1965), p. 2.
2 Malcolm Bradbury and James McFarlane, "The Name and Nature of Modernism" in Malcolm Bradbury and James McFarlane, eds., *Modernism: 1890-1930* (Harmondsworth: Penguin Books, Ltd.), pp. 19-55.
3 Irving Howe, ed., *The Idea of the Modern in Literature and the Arts* (New York: Horizon Press, 1967), p. 12.
4 Interestingly, the term *psychology* (in its Latin cognate) only gained some currency with the appearance of Christian Wolff's *Psychologia empirica* (1732) and *Psychologia Rationalis* (1734).
5 MacIntyre, p. 111.
6 See especially Chapter 7 of MacIntyre's *After Virtue.*
7 Michael Ondaatje, *Running in the Family* (Toronto: McClelland and Stewart, 1982), p. 129.
8 Robert Buttel, *Wallace Stevens: The making of "Harmonium"* (Princeton, N.J.: Princeton University Press, 1967), p. 191.

9 An engaging portrait of Dewdney is offered in David McFadden's "The Twilight of Self-Consciousness" from David Helwig, ed., *The Human Elements*, pp. 78-96.

10 Paul Feyerabend, *Science in a Free Society* (London: NLB, 1978), p. 64.

11 Ondaatje, *Running in the Family*, pp. 53-54.

12 Ibid., p. 26.

13 Ibid., p. 206.

14 Perry M. Nodelman, "Photographs of Billy the Kid," *Canadian Literature*, No. 87, Winter 1980, p. 69.

15 Ondaatje, *Running in the Family*, p. 37.

16 Ibid., pp. 84-86, 99-101.

17 Ibid., p. 68.

18 R.G. Collingwood, *The Idea of History*, ed. T.M. Knox (London: Oxford University Press, 1956), p. 218.

19 Ondaatje, *Running in the Family*, p. 27.

20 Ibid., pp. 186-187.

21 Ibid., p. 179.

22 Ibid., p. 182.

Works by Michael Ondaatje / Selected Criticism

Publications

The Dainty Monsters. Toronto: The Coach House Press, 1967.

The Man with Seven Toes. Toronto: The Coach House Press, 1969.

Leonard Cohen. Toronto: McClelland and Stewart Ltd., 1970.

The Collected Works of Billy the Kid: Left Handed Poems. Toronto: House of Anansi Press, 1970.

Editor, *The Broken Ark: A Book of Beasts.* Ottawa: Oberon Press, 1971.

Rat Jelly. Toronto: The Coach House Press, 1973.

"O'Hagan's Rough-Edged Chronicle," *Canadian Literature,* No. 61, Summer 1974, pp. 24-31. Also in: George Woodcock, ed., *The Canadian Novel in the Twentieth Century: Essays from 'Canadian Literature'* (Toronto: McClelland and Stewart Ltd., 1975), pp. 276-284.

" 'How Long Since I Was Sauntering across Piazza Erbe in Verona?' " and "Dashiell" in "Outlaws, Light and Avocadoes: Poems," *The Canadian Forum,.* LIV March 1975, 24-26.

Coming Through Slaughter. Toronto: House of Anansi Press, 1976.

Editor, *Personal Fictions: Stories by Munro, Wiebe, Thomas, and Blaise.* Toronto: Oxford University Press, 1977.

Elimination Dance. Ilderton, Ont.: Nairn Publishing House, 1978.

There's a Trick with a Knife I'm Learning to Do. Toronto: McClelland and Stewart, 1979.

Editor, *The Long Poem Anthology.* Toronto: The Coach House Press, 1979.

"Where Cows Burn Like Newsprint," *The Canadian Forum,* LX. April 1980, 42-43.

"Cut Down the Middle" in *Tasks of Passion: Dennis Lee at Mid-Career,* ed. Karen Mulholland et al. Toronto: Descant Editions, 1982, pp. 20-21.

Tin Roof. Lantzville, B.C.: Island Writing Series, 1982.

Running in the Family. Toronto: McClelland and Stewart, 1982.
"Pacific letter," "Translations of My Postcards:," and "The River
Neighbour" (poems) in *Ethos*, 1 (Summer 1983), 19-21.

Films

Sons of Captain Poetry, 1970.
Carry on Crime and Punishment, 1972.
The Clinton Special, 1974.

Selected Criticism and Interviews

Abley, Mark. "Bone Beneath Skin," *Maclean's*, xcii (April 23,
    1979), 62-63.
———. "The Past Is Another Country," *Maclean's*, xcv (October
    11, 1982), 66.
Adachi, Ken. "A Memoir Illumined by Imagination," *The Toronto
    Star*, October 9, 1982, p. F10.
Balliett, Whitney. "Lalla and Mervyn," *The New Yorker*, lviii
    (December 27, 1982), 76-77.
Barbour, Douglas. "All That Poetry Should Be," *The Canadian
    Forum*, lix (June / July 1979), 34-35.
Blott, Anne. " 'Stories to Finish': *The Collected Works of Billy the
    Kid*," *Studies in Canadian Literature*, ii (Summer 1977), 188-
    202.
Broyard, Anatole. "New Woman, Old Jazz, Hemingway," *The New
    York Times Book Review*, April 24, 1977, p. 14.
Brydon, Diana. "Making the Present Continuous," *Canadian
    Literature*, No. 86, Autumn 1980, pp. 99-100.
Conlogue, Ray. "Ondaatje's Ego Smothers 'Coming Through
    Slaughter,' " *The Globe and Mail*, cxxxvi (January 11, 1980), 15.
Davey, Frank. *From There to Here: A Guide to English-Canadian
    Literature Since 1960* (Erin, Ont.: Press Porcepic, 1974), pp.
    222-227.
French, William. Untitled review of *Running in the Family*, *The
    Globe and Mail*, cxxxix (October 9, 1982), E15.
Green, Benny. "All That Jazz," *The Spectator*, ccxliii (September 8,
    1979), 25.
Hancock, Geoff. Untitled review of *Coming Through Slaughter*, *The
    Malahat Review*, No. 44, October 1977, pp. 140-142.
Helwig, David. "From Ondaatje to Lee: Words That Live As
    Poetry," *Saturday Night*, xciv (November 1979), 58-61.

Kahn, Sy. Untitled review of *The Dainty Monsters, The Far Point,* No. 1, Fall / Winter 1968, pp. 70-76.

Kareda, Urjo. "An Immigrant's Song," *Saturday Night,* XCVIII (December 1983), 44-51.

Kertzer, J.M. "On Death and Dying: *The Collected Works of Billy the Kid,*" *English Studies in Canada,* I (Spring 1975), 86-96.

———. Untitled review of *Coming through Slaughter, The Fiddlehead,* No. 113, Spring 1977, pp. 126-128.

Kroetsch, Robert. "The Exploding Porcupine: Violence of form in English-Canadian Fiction," *Open Letter,* fifth series, No. 4, Spring 1983, pp. 57-64.

Lancashire, David. "Play about Jazzman Takes Dramatic Licence," *The Globe and Mail,* CXXXVI (January 2, 1980), 13.

Lane, M. Travis. "Dream as History," *The Fiddlehead,* No. 86, August / October 1970, pp. 158-162.

Lee, Dennis. *Savage Fields: An Essay in Literature and Cosmology* (Toronto: House of Anansi Press, 1977).

MacLulich, T.D. "Ondaatje's Mechanical Boy: Portrait of the Artist as Photographer," *Mosaic,* XIV (Spring 1981), 107-119.

McNally, Paul. Untitled review of *There's a Trick With a Knife I'm Learning to Do: Poems 1963-78, Queen's Quarterly,* LXXXVI (winter 1979 / 1980), 720-721.

MacSkimming, Roy. "The Good Jazz," *Canadian Literature,* No. 73, Summer 1977, pp. 92-94.

Manna, No. 1, March 1972, pp. 19-22. Untitled interview.

Mukherjee, Bharati. "Ondaatje's Sri Lanka Is Prospero's Isle," *Quill & Quire,* XLVIII (October 1982), 30.

Nodelman, Perry M. "Photographs of Billy the Kid," *Canadian Literature,* No. 87, Winter 1980, pp. 68-79.

Oughton, John. "Sane Assassin," *Books in Canada,* XII (June / July 1983), 7-10.

Owens, Judith. " 'I Send You a Picture': Ondaatje's Portrait of Billy the Kid," *Studies in Canadian Literature,* VIII (Summer 1983), 117-139.

Pearce, Jon, ed. "Moving to the Clear: Michael Ondaatje" in *Twelve Voices: Interviews with Canadian Poets* (Ottawa: Borealis Press, 1980), pp. 130-143.

Prato, Ed. "A Net Full of Ondaatje," *Canadian Literature,* No. 87, Winter 1980, pp. 103-105.

Reid, Christopher. "Whimsically Busy," *The Times Literary Supplement,* No. 4,191, July 29, 1983, p. 811.

Roosevelt, Karyl. Untitled review of *The Collected Works of Billy the Kid*, *The New York Times Book Review*, November 17, 1974, pp. 48-49. Sarker, Eileen. "Michael Ondaatje's *Billy the Kid*: The Esthetics of Violence," *World Literature Written in English*, XII (November 1973), 230-239.

Scobie, Stephen. "*Coming Through Slaughter*: Fictional Magnets and Spider's Webbs," *Essays on Canadian Writing*, No. 12, Fall 1978, pp. 5-22.

———. "His Legend a Jungle Sleep," *Canadian Literature*, No. 76, Spring 1978, pp. 6-21.

———. "Two Authors in Search of a Character," *Canadian Literature*, No. 54, Autumn 1972, pp. 37-55. Also in: George Woodcock, ed., *Poets and Critics: Essays from 'Canadian Literature' 1966-1974* (Toronto: Oxford University Press, 1974), pp. 225-246.

Solecki, Sam. "An interview with Michael Ondaatje," *Rune*, No. 2, Spring 1975, pp. 39-54.

———. "Dementia Praecox, Paranoid Type," *The Canadian Forum*, LVI (December 1976-January 1977), 46-47.

———. "Making and Destroying: Michael Ondaatje's *Coming Through Slaughter* and Extremist Art," *Essays on Canadian Writing*, No. 12, Fall 1978, pp. 24-47.

———. "Nets and Chaos: The Poetry of Michael Ondaatje," *Studies in Canadian Literature*, II (Winter 1977), 36-48.

———. "Point Blank: Narrative in Michael Ondaatje's *The Man with Seven Toes*," *Canadian Poetry*, No. 6, Spring / Summer 1980, pp. 14-24.

———. "Sharpening His Act," *Books in Canada*, VIII (June 1979), 11.

Smith, Patricia Keeney. "Michael Ondaatje: A Poet Sets the Stage," *Performing Arts in Canada*, XVII (Spring 1980), 30-33.

Watson, Sheila. "Michael Ondaatje: The Mechanization of Death," *White Pelican*, II (1972), 56-64. Also in: *Open Letter*, third series, No. 1, pp. 158-166.

Witten, Mark. "Billy, Buddy, and Michael," *Books in Canada*, VI (June / July 1977), 9-10, 12-13.

Wyman, Max. "Billy the Kid, Baby-Faced Billy, Where Did You Go Plumb Wrong?" *The Vancouver Sun*, March 3, 1977, p. 31.

Young, Alan. "Particular Horrors," *The Times Literary Supplement*, No. 4,091, August 28, 1981, p. 988.

Index

X